Songs and Dreams

Songs and Dreams

by seeking we are found

NEILL REILLY

LINDISFARNE BOOKS | 2017

Lindisfarne Books
An imprint of SteinerBooks / Anthroposophic Press, Inc.
610 Main St., Great Barrington, MA 01230
www.steinerbooks.org

Design: Jens Jensen
Cover image: Candles,
Cathedral Nostra Signora dell'Orto,
Chiavari, Italy © by Neill Reilly

Library of Congress Control Number: 2017937761
ISBN: 978-1-58420-962-1 (paperback)
ISBN: 978-1-58420-963-8 (ebook)

Printed in the United States of America

Contents

Dedicated to

Gladys O'Neill Reilly

and

Thomas Joseph Reilly

I would like to offer special thanks to J. Bruce Murphy, Paul O'Leary, Andy Leaf, and Lee Lecraw for their editing and their encouragement of the production of *Songs and Dreams*.

"If today you hear His voice, harden not your hearts."

(Psalm 95:7–8)

Foreword

J. Bruce Murphy

T he songs (over a hundred), and dreams (thirteen) come over a twenty-three-year period, from 1994 to 2017. In a certain sense, they have reached their majority of twenty-one years of age. Probably the time is ripe for them to sound forth into the wider world.

My aunt, Sister St. Theresa said, "Obviously these [*Songs and Dreams*] were written by a Catholic boy." It should be noted however that she should have qualified her statement. These songs and dreams come to us from (through?) a Catholic boy for sure, but particularly through one who is also decidedly Irish Catholic.

In his foreword to Christopher Bamford's *The Voice of the Eagle,* Thomas Moore refers to "the Irish sensibility, where the veil between the holy and the ordinary is thinner than elsewhere else on Earth" (p. 9). This feeling echoes through these songs. Bamford writes in the introduction to his book that the Celts "lived a life of spiritual freedom verging on anarchy." He quotes Jean Markale:

> The essence of Celtic philosophy would appear to be a search for individual freedom, not based on egoism, but founded in the belief that each person is special and therefore different from others, that behavior cannot be modeled on a pattern created by others. (ibid., p. 23)

Songs and Dreams strikes this Celtic note placing great emphasis on individual freedom. This is the chord that is struck by these *Songs*: one of an "intuition of *the divine vocation of freedom*" (ibid., p. 31), and "the fierce spiritualism rampant in Ireland" (ibid., p. 37). At the heart of the mystery of "Celtic Christianity," Bamford identifies a "sevenfold gift," the last of which is the "implacable ability not only to tolerate contradiction and paradox, but also sheer chaos and confusion, and to do so with a smile…this gives the Irish their lyricism and their sense of humor. It is a humor of renewed innocence" (ibid., p. 51). The lilt of this humor and laughter floats across the songs.

It is also evident that the *Songs* are written by someone who is familiar with what it means to be a salesman. See *Who can refuse the Lord?* (page 27), with its references to the product, the pitch, the demonstration, and the guarantee. The details in the dream about George Clooney reflect the salesman's perspective. You can see the classic sales techniques: assume the win, close the deal, and move in closer to force a decision and commitment from the client. The picture of the Devil in this dream is spot on. In *Karmic Relationships*, Rudolf Steiner says, "If ever we let ourselves in for a discussion with Ahriman, we would inevitably be shattered by the logical conclusiveness, the magnificent certainty of aim with which he manipulates his arguments" (vol. 3, p. 126). This sounds like the one described in this dream.

It is remarkable that the writer, of all people, has songs and that so often these songs urge him to be still and listen. That songs and singing are his medium stretches credulity. "You who love to hear the sound of your own voice" and "Be Quiet. Listen" are in *Learn to listen* (page 78). "Be still. Be quiet" is in *Be still* (page 60).

Christopher Bamford writes, "It is only in and through the Word, the *primordial singing principle*…that the true religion is to be found" (*The Voice of the Eagle*, p. 123). Singing, listening, and being still do not come to mind when thinking of Reilly's strengths and attributes. Yet, the *Songs* are here. Go figure.

In his book *An Astronaut's Guide to Life on Earth,* Chris Hadfield quotes singer–songwriter Neil Young: "I never write songs. I just write them down. If the song isn't flowing through you of its own accord, it might be a good idea to wait until it is...be careful not to judge a song until it's finished...so it doesn't get poisoned or stunted" (p. 227). *Paintings of the Soul* (page 32) states:

> They are paintings of the soul,
> but I am not the artist. I am the canvas.
> Other times there are words and phrases that
> suggest meanings that I don't fully comprehend.
> Curiously I often don't read what is given.

I guess the light sounds (yes light sounds) through whatever medium there is available to it, even through an Irish, Catholic, salesman, athlete. It must also be said that Neill is an anthroposophist, or better said, is someone who counts Rudolf Steiner as his teacher and friend. In *From Jesus to Christ* (lecture 4, Oct. 8, 1911), Steiner says:

> Many people can approach the Pauline Epistles feeling themselves ready to understand this or that, because in the spiritual world it meets their opened eyes. Should they wish at the same time to understand another passage, perhaps quite close to it, they may not be able to do so. It is necessary today to curb this thirst for knowledge. One should rather say to oneself: Grace has brought me to a certain number of truths. I will wait patiently until further truths flow to me. Today there is really more need for a certain passive attitude than there was perhaps twenty years ago. This attitude is

necessary because our minds must completely ripen to allow truths to enter us in their right form. This is a practical lesson regarding investigation of the spiritual worlds, especially in relation to the Christ Event. It is fundamentally wrong when people think they can grasp at what ought to stream toward them in a certain passive way. *For we must be conscious that we can be what we ought to be only insofar as we are judged worthy by the spiritual powers to be this or that. All that we can do through meditation, contemplation, and so forth is really done only to open our eyes—not to seize the truths but to let them come to us, for we may not run after them.*[*]

The italics are mine. This quotation struck me as very similar to this song on page III:

> Spiritual activity is incense,
> rising to the heavens.
> Spiritual activity declares our existence
>   and location to spiritual beings
> including the so-called dead.
> Spiritual activity is a buoy.
> It creates a marker for where we are.
> Once the spiritual world knows we exist and where we are,
> it can shower grace upon grace upon us,
> Spiritual activity is the free act that connects us
>   to the spiritual world.
> We are open and the spiritual world fills us up.
> By seeking, we are found.

The light that shines (and sounds) through these songs gives rise to a picture of a "muscular Christianity" (a phrase from the film *Chariots of Fire*). For instance, in *A Few good players* from St. Patrick's Day, 1996,: "All we need are a few good players" (page 23); or *Pray*

---

[*] Translations have been revised for modern, gender-inclusive language.

Hard: "Pray like an aggressive football player. Tackle Me with your love" (page 31); or in *The Veil,* nine years later: "But our end goal is clear—to run freely" (page 64),; and most especially the Michaelic "I need troops for my army" (*Troops for My Army,* page 47); and "the battle is fierce because it is so important" (*Epiphanies,* page 85). He is in good company. Referring to his book *Intuitive Thinking as a Spiritual Path: A Philosophy of Freedom,* Rudolf Steiner said, "It was necessary to try to write a book that would represent, *in an energetic way,*" his viewpoint regarding the question of human freedom (*Becoming the Archangel Michael's Companions,* p. 39).

Reading too many of the songs makes me feel a little bit seasick. I find that a little goes a long way. However, I do not advocate for several volumes or wholesale abbreviation. One does not simply read *Songs and Dreams.* One experiences them. So, you may as well take your time and let the *Songs* take their time. For instance in *Experience the Word* (page 41):

> Don't just read these words.
> Experience them.
> They are meant to open you up.

The experience is pictorial. It is wide awake, but it is not the usual, everyday way of seeing, feeling, thinking, or being. For example, in *Dark to the Mind, Radiant to the Soul* (page 47):

> Much of what I say you cannot understand.
> It is not meant to be understood; it is meant to be lived.

The *Songs* are not dreamy or sentimental: "I'm not talking about Hallmark greeting cards" (*Love and Karma,* page 54), and they are poetic: "Clarity has been seduced by sloth" (*Epiphanies,* page 85).

The songs, when experienced, are actually very practical and down to Earth. For example, "Right here, right now" from *Right*

Here, Right Now (page 38), or "Join Me in the here and now," from *There is Ordinary Time* (page 17). They are factual and real. "Be a realist, live in the spirit," from *Live in the Spirit* (page 10); or see *Paintings of the Soul* (page 32) for "the real challenge." The many references in the *Songs* to seeing "Christ in the other" are practical, real, actual spiritual exercises. The question of freedom and the ego and egoism is a thread that runs through the entire series of the songs. The ego is mentioned in *Alleluia,* the first song on page 1, and in a later song, *Spiritual Elitism* (page 115). Go figure.

The dreams are cinematic—the cathedral with the columns, the cave with its altars, the knights and battles, even to an appearance by George Clooney. All the scenes are worthy of an award-winning screenwriter. One of my favorite scenes is in *The Correct Approach* (page 24).

I am especially fond of *Thomas and Paul* (page 94). It is a song of "unbiased observations," or perhaps more properly of epistemology. The connection of Christ with cognition is beautifully pictured.

The songs speak frequently of the inner life. They also boldly proclaim the presence of the Christ in our outer world. The song *Rejoice* (page 86) celebrates the power and strength of the Cosmic Christ all around us in the great world and Christ's protection of us from the assaults of our adversaries.

> Rejoice!
> We rejoice when He calls us by our individual name.
> We rejoice when He leads us into His promised land.
> We rejoice when He is above us.
> We rejoice when He is below us.
> We rejoice when He is around us.
> We rejoice when He is within us.
> Rejoice!

The similarity of these lines (as well as other lines in the songs) to the prayer *St. Patrick's Breastplate* is clear. It, too, speaks about the Christ within, but also about the Christ in the world around us and seeks the protection of Christ from all those who seek to do us harm.

Songs and Dreams echos the firm conviction of St. Patrick—that the power of the Christ will not only suffice, but will also triumph and yield blessings unimagined. The help for which we long is confidently expected and celebrated.

In conclusion, these songs are good medicine for the health of soul but are best in small doses—a little goes a long way. There is more here than meets the eye, so plant the seed and see what grows. Experience the songs. As the song *Step out of the Darkness* says: "And just as all plants grow toward the Sun, all humans grow toward the Son" (page 104).

These are my favorite one-liners and pertinent questions:

Alleluia, "All of life comes down to either Alleluia or *Non Serviam*." (p. 1)

The Direct Approach, "Would you hire someone to hug your child?" (p. 2)

Spiritual Agents, "I did not call you to be librarians, referring people to books on the spirit." (p. 8)

Live in the Spirit, "Be a realist, live in the spirit." (p. 11)

I Am with You Always, "'I am with you always even unto the end of the Earth.' Did you think I was kidding?" (p. 18)

Bring Me to Everyone You Meet, "Your business meeting or chance encounter may be an opportunity for Me. Don't blow the chance!" (p. 19)

A Few Good Players, "I could use your help in this matter" and "All we need are a few good players." (p. 23)

How Do You Spend Your Time? "I could use some good friends to help Me with My task." (p. 23)

The Correct Approach, "The Direct Approach is interesting, but we are concerned with the Correct Approach." (p. 24)

Who Can Refuse the Lord? "Think of Him as the best salesman in the world." (p. 27)

Faith, "With faith you can see the real world." (p. 58)

The Veil "...our end goal is clear—to run freely." (p. 64)

An Internal Electric Storm, "This is a game of spiritual, electric tag." (p. 68)

Karma, Fate, Sins, or Physics, "You break it, you own it." (p. 70)

Learn to Listen, "You, who love to hear the sound of your own voice." (p. 78)

A Dream about the Devil Who Looked like George Clooney, "To the best of my knowledge, my father never lied to me." "And neither has my heavenly Father." (p. 84)

Epiphanies, "Clarity has been seduced by sloth." (p. 85)

Epiphanies, "The battle is fierce because it is so important." (p. 85)

Thomas and Paul, the allusions to *The Philosophy of Freedom*: "unbiased observations"; "Let the concept emerge from the percept"; "We often lack the concepts to unite with the percepts." (p. 95)

Armor of Light, "We have sworn allegiance to the Light." (p. 97)

Love Makes All Things Anew, "Love makes all things anew including dogma and ideology." (p. 98)

Catharsis Ain't Fun. (p. 103)

Seek and Ye Shall Find, another reference to *The Philosophy of Freedom* "unprejudiced observation." (p. 107)

With God all Things Are Possible, yet another reference to *The Philosophy of Freedom*: "...like Christ, the knowing doer." (p. 110)

Spiritual Activity Is Incense, "By seeking, we are found." (p. 111)

Introduction

My mother, Gladys O'Neill Reilly, was a great storyteller. Consequently she spoke a great deal. Mary was one of her best friends. The two would talk over tea in their respective kitchens for hours. My mother died in 1984; Mary died in 1985. Lori, Mary's daughter, was so distraught at her mother's Funeral Mass that Blayney, her father, recommended that she stay the night with him at their home. She agreed and went solemnly up to her bedroom.

The next day, Lori came down to the kitchen and was so changed in appearance that Blayney asked her what had happened.

Lori stated she did not believe what had occurred to her. Mary had come to her during a dream and told her to be calm. She assured Lori that she was fine; there was no need for concern. Lori was immediately relieved. Mary said there was only one problem in the afterlife. Lori asked what it was. Mary replied, "Gladys won't shut up!"

Lori told me that experience and we laughed very hard. We both knew it rang true. Lori's experience proved two points.

> Our so-called dead love us and want to stay connected.
> The spiritual world has a sense of humor.

We all have regular dreams. We can also have experiences that are more than dreams. We remember them like waking experiences.

We are conscious during them. They are indicative of spiritual reality. Likewise we all have regular, sense-bound thoughts. Once in a while we can be gifted with an intuition that is more real than a physical experience. It is sense-free. It endures.

In 1994 I had a horrendous nightmare dream experience. The devil was chasing me. If he tagged me, he owned me and could force me to do his bidding. The only way to get free was to tag him and then run before he re-tagged me. We were constantly watching out or searching for one another. It was spy vs. spy in my soul. It was extremely frightening to be tagged and caught by him. The solution was in some ways scarier. It really made him angry if he was outsmarted, if I was tagging him and running free. He would redouble his efforts to tag me again. Our persistence mirrored one another. This never-ending game became weary and led to near submission. Then the realization hit me and the implications of servitude to the devil would propel me to get free again. This made him madder than mad.

At the end of the sequence, I awoke, clearly troubled. My wife listened to my experience and kindly stated, "But Neill, you know who you are and where you are going." It was like a sunrise. She was right. I started praising God with an internal Alleluia. After a short while, an inner song came to me. It was more of an internal experience and a soul mood or a dim image with a few words. Amazed, I got up and wrote it down before the images were lost.

I read the first two of the following songs at a meeting with friends. Julie looked at me and said. "Well, now that you have opened that door, you are going to get a lot more." I couldn't understand what she was saying or how prophetic or insightful it was.

There is a correlation between waking experiences in a sleep state and inner experiences in a waking state. Both have an awakened consciousness. It is critical to understand that these songs are halting attempts to put into words inner events that are experienced in a waking consciousness. Inner experiences are filtered into images, ideas, and feelings and then translated into words. This is a derivative process that condenses activity into words.

The polar opposite process occurs for the reader. If the words resonate with the reader, the reader then recreates images, ideas, and feelings. The reader can possibly have a very similar inner activity. Each reader has a creative process that has a life of its own. Ironically the individual creates the inner activity, but it can lead to a universal experience.

Songs and Dreams

All of life comes down to either Alleluia or *Non Serviam*.
All the heavenly hosts of angels
want to sing Alleluia with you.
They want to sing through you.
This is the song of creation.
All the dark forces want you
to shout *Non Serviam*.
They want you to stay caught,
imprisoned in your ego.
This is a decision you must make
every day, every minute.

T<small>HIS</small> D<small>AY</small>

When the Lord created this day,
He had you in mind.
Take it, seize it, squeeze it.
Let it unfold like a rose before you,
petal by petal, minute by minute.
Find out why He created this day for you.

THE DIRECT APPROACH   3/27/94, PALM SUNDAY

The direct approach is the only way to Me.
How else can it be?
Do you not long to look directly
into your loved one's eyes?
Would you hire someone to hug your child?
Would you choose an intermediary over a loved one?
Why do you think it is any different for Me?
I long for your direct gaze into My eyes.

LIKE A THIEF IN THE NIGHT

Be prepared.
Changes are coming, hard and fast.
Be strong!
You will endure.
Be calm.
I will be with you always.

ALL PATHS LEAD TO ME

The short and the long.
The steep and the easy.
Some paths intersect, some are parallel.
Others are dead ends,
and force a new beginning.
Don't worry, I am the compass.

DO MY WILL

I have a task for you.
To do My will.
How will you know My will?

By listening.
Listen to My song.
You can hear it the morning,
when the birds begin to sing.
Isn't it lovely that I awaken you.
with the song of the morning dove?
I want to gently pull you out of your slumber
as a mother gently wakes her child.
Not only do I want you to listen,
I want you to sing.
Every word, every thought and gesture
has its tone.
Is your song in tune with Me?
Listen.
Then sing.

IN THE BEGINNING

In the beginning was the Singer,
And the Singer sang His Song.
And the Singer was in the Song.
And the Song was in the Singer.
The Singer and the Song are One.

TRIAL AND TRIBULATION   3/28/94

This is a time of trial and tribulation.
Be prepared!
Everyone will be tested.
You will fall again and again.
The devil is mighty and determined.
After you fall, rise up, try again,
even though you have just failed,
Sing!

Child's Play

Treat your life as a child does, play
Even pain can be seen as play.
Watch brave children play through their pain.
I have come to redeem pain,
by making it meaningful.

Most People Are Preoccupied with Family 3/30/94

Work, sports, or money.
Spend some of that time with Me.
Compared to the Sun,
the gardener spends only
a few minutes in the garden.
You should be the gardener of your own soul,
tilling it, planting seeds, weeding it.
I will shine on you,
and you will bring forth much fruit.

A tree's branches reach only

A tree's branches reach only
as far as its roots allow it.
Likewise, you can only reach the Father
by being rooted in Me.

When We Praise the Lord 3/31/94, Holy Thursday

When we praise the Lord, we are in His presence.
By singing His praises,
we open our hearts to Him.
It is as if a spell has been broken.
He is able to emanate out of our hearts
and manifest Himself.

MY RACE TOWARD YOUR HEART   4/1/94, GOOD FRIDAY

My race toward your heart
is sometimes a sprint,
fast and strong.
Other times it is a marathon,
patient and enduring.
It all depends on what's best for you.

NATURE IS IN A FETAL STATE

Slumbering, waiting for man to be
a midwife to her rebirth.
Then she could display the full glory of God.
It is man's quest on Earth to be the midwife,
but first he must be reborn himself.

I SING

I sing
He listens.
He sings.
I listen.

THE LORD WANTS YOU TO STEER

The Lord wants you to steer
your boat right into the storm.
He wants you to point your skis
straight down the mountain.
He dislikes you going from side to side.
Be bold!
He would rather you be foolish
than fickle in your love for Him.

A Still Pond   4/5/94

A still pond reflects the beauty of the sky
A raging river sweeps all along.
Make your mind still
so that it reflects on Me.
Then let Me rage through your heart.

My Blood   4/10/94

My blood had to join with the Earth.
The crucifixion allowed this to happen.
I incarnated into the flesh through Jesus.
I incarnated into the Earth through My Crucifixion.
My karma is one with this world.
"I shall be with you always,
even to the end of the world." (Matt. 28:20)
My hands were nailed to the Cross.
My side was ripped open by a spear.
This had to happen.
This helped My blood enter the Earth.
These wounds of My body are direct openings
    to the spiritual world.
Through them My ego flows directly into earthly life.
My pain and My wounds are the doors to the spiritual world.
Through these doors flow the light of the Spirit Sun.
This is why I radiated light after the Resurrection.
The light streams through these openings.

Now Is the Time

Now is the time for Me to incarnate into you.
What action, thought or feeling
is not connected with Me?

No matter how trivial or insignificant
it may seem to you.
All your actions have a tone.
Let them all ring true.
Let them sing of Me.

INVITE ME INTO YOUR HEART

Unless you invite Me into your heart,
it is very difficult for Me to enter.
I can knock at the door,
but you must open the door.
The invitation must be sincere and heartfelt.

THE DIRECT APPROACH TO ME

Some fear the direct approach to Me.
They think they are not ready,
or not holy enough.
Others fear that if they open themselves to the spirit,
dark forces may enter.
As if dark forces are not trying all the time.
These doubts and concerns are very human.
Remember I doubted My Father's love on the cross,
"Father, Father, why hast Thou abandoned Me?" (Matt. 27:46)
Fear not the direct approach.

REMEMBER ME

Let your songs be your sword,
and your memories of Me your shield.
You are not alone.

THE MIDST OF ETERNITY

We are in the midst of eternity.
The world is in a state of becoming.
The Lord has asked us to help Him
recreate the world by doing His will.

THE GENTLE PATH   5/7/94

Be patient.
Be calm.
Be kind.
Prepare a place in your heart for Me.
For some this is very difficult.
Therefore, it is even more important.

THE LORD IS VERY PATIENT

He waits until we understand.
He takes His time.
His approach is gentle and slow.
He does not force Himself upon us.
He awaits our readiness.

SPIRITUAL AGENTS   5/13/94, ASCENSION THURSDAY

I did not choose you to be librarians,
referring people to books on the spirit.
I want you to be spiritual agents,
active participants in My work.
Do not proselytize.
Act!

Open Yourself to Me   5/28/94

If you open yourself to Me,
My countenance can shine through you.
As a mirror reflects the Sun
or a bead of water the world around it,
you can carry My image to others.
Shine on!

Dream 1: Recollection of a 1970 Dream   6/10/94

I dreamt of a steel fence, tall and black with points at the top. Behind the fence was a green lawn, verdant and tranquil. Off in the distant, left-hand corner of the field, the Sun shone brightly.

I walked to the fence to gaze on the Sun, which seemed to transform itself into a lamb. My hands rested on the cold steel fence. I became engrossed and wanted to get closer as the lamb started to turn into a cross.

Out of the corner of my eye, I noticed a small man in a majestic, long, blue robe walk, more float, down the left side of the fence. He turned the corner where the two sides joined into a right angle. He approached me, but my attention was on the transformation of the lamb into a cross. I was so engrossed that I parted the steel bars as if they were butter. I stared at the cross and started to step through the bars.

Just as I had demonstrated immense strength, the little man came by my right side and touched my right elbow. It was if he had a magnet. He moved me away from the fence and started to talk to me. His speech was incomprehensible. His blue gown was decorated with archaic symbols. I was totally confused and felt uneasy. He walked on my left side and kept talking. Finally, I asked, "But how do I know that you are a Christian?" With that his first finger on his right hand pointed to his left hand. He raised the ring finger on his left hand On this finger there was a figure of a fish. With that I felt immense relief and continued to walk with him.

The Fence of Our Ego 6/10/94, 24 years later

Your ego is a fence that surrounds you.
It protects you from outside influences.
It also limits and constrains you.
If you try to break through to the other side,
you can harm yourself.
You must find the gate to the fence.
It is located at the center of your heart.
By praying and meditating, you can open this gate.

Sacred Vessels 6/13/94

You are all vessels, sacred vessels
No matter how battered you look,
you are the beneficiaries of My sacrifice.
My blood is in you.
Don't search for the Holy Grail.
You are it.

Live in the Spirit

Take what the Lord gives you.
He knows what is best.
Don't be a fatalist,

resigned to defeat.
Be a realist,
live in the spirit

How Can You Doubt the Direct Approach?   7/24/94

Do you fear it?
Remember what I said.
"Behold, I stand at the door and knock;
    if any one hears my voice and opens the door,
    I will come in to him and eat with him
    and he with me." (Rev. 3:20)
Do you think that I was kidding?

Do Not Think of the Direct Approach
as New or Mystical   8/4/94

I incarnated into the flesh to be with you.
I died to free you from death.
I rose to give you new life.
All the Christian rituals lead to a Direct Approach.
Communion is a Direct Union with me.
"I am the Bread of Life," is not a metaphor.
It is a spiritual reality.
All prayer, all meditation aim at the Direct Approach.
The first goal of ritual and prayer is union with Me.
The second goal is union with your fellow man.
"Thou shalt love the Lord thy God with all thy heart,
    and with all thy soul, and with all thy strength,
    and with all thy mind; and thy neighbor as thyself."
                                        (Luke 10:27)

Good Works Are Wings 8/19/94

Your prayers, meditations and good works are wings
that carry you through spiritual space.
First your wings need to be exercised.
Just as a young bird flaps its wings in the nest,
so must you.
Your flapping is not in vain.
It is the exercise that builds strength.
Only through acquired strength can you fly on your own.
This is why you are on the Earth,
to learn how to fly.

Spiritual Vision 9/7/94

The difficulty with spiritual vision is that
spiritual realities are not static.
They metamorphose.
Watch water coalesce on a leaf.
Slowly it collects together.
Then it quickly forms a drop.
Then the drop hangs on the lip of the leaf
and forms itself into a sphere.
Then it releases from the leaf and falls.
A static view of this process
would be limited and one sided.
Spiritual images seem to be made of water.
They change shape, sometimes quickly, sometimes slowly.
It is hard to get a good read.
Clear and patient apprehension is critical.

INVITE THE GUEST   9/10/94

If you want the Guest to come to your home,
you must invite Him.
If you invite Him, He will come.
If you don't invite Him, how will He know He is welcomed?
If you become acquainted, He will invite you to His home.
Who knows? You might become best of friends.

IT IS HARD TO FORGIVE   9/18/94

It is one of My most difficult requests.
Forgive all!
This is the true cross,
to die for the other.
A part of you dies when you forgive.
It is painful and hard to do.
When you forgive, you are reborn.

THE LIGHT OF CHRIST   11/3/94

The light of Christ illuminates and warms the human spirit.
But most important of all, the light transforms the spirit.
A seed, buried deep below the ground, grows toward
the warmth and light of the Sun.
The human spirit, buried deep inside man,
grows toward the warmth and light of Christ.
In this turning toward the light,
the human spirit is transformed.
This new man is enlightened by Christ.

BEARERS OF THE LIGHT

This is not something new.
It stretches far back in time and far forward.
It is a long and unbroken chain of hope.
We are all connected to it
and march consciously to support it.
We are united by this call to bear the Light in this age
and pass it on to the next.

THE MORE YOU LOVE ME, THE MORE I'LL TEST YOU   12/11/94

The more I test you, the more I love you.
Does that seem cruel or unfair?
There is pain for the mother and the child during birth.
No one would advocate that the child stay in the womb
and avoid the pain.
Love your pain and troubles.
They help you to become reborn.
You could be lame.
You could be deaf.
Whatever your problems are, your children or your work,
    love them.
The reason that they bother you so much
is that they are so important to you.
Your problems are why you are here.

WE ARE I AM

When two or more are gathered, is it still "I AM"?
Or is it "We are"?
Could it be "We am"?
Possibly it is "We are I AM"?

SHOUTS AND WHISPERS   12/26/94

Sometimes He shouts, most often He whispers
in a voice so soft that He forces me to be still and calm.
It can be a word, a phrase, or an image.
It attracts me as gravity attracts a falling stone to the Earth.
I find a space within me, that I didn't know existed,
is filled with ideas I never thought about.

YOU ARE NOT ALONE   1/14/95

I, your Lord and your God, am here with you.
Rejoice!

WHAT A MYSTERY THE CROSS IS!

What a mystery the Cross is!
Without it there is no resurrection.
Each of us must bear his own cross.
In order to be reborn as the new Adam,
we must die.
We must learn to love our cross,
no matter how heavy it is.

I WANT YOU TO SEE ME IN ALL PEOPLE   2/15/95

I want you to see Me in all people.
Many will say they cannot do it.
Try.
Try again.
If you fail, imagine that you can see Me in another person.
Surely, anyone can try this.
Do not expect failure.
Try.

The Fat Man with the Greasy Hair 3/6/95

The fat man with the greasy hair
in the subway car is your brother.
How hard it is for you to get past the accidental.
Strive for the essential.
Look for the eternal.
I am as much a part of him
as I am a part of you.
If you can see Me in him,
you can help both of you to become free.

Paul and Damascus 3/24/95

Imagine if Paul had kept his experience on the road
    to Damascus to himself.
There could be no Christianity in the West.
But it was impossible for him to keep quiet.
The essence of the Christian experience is to share
    the good word with others.
The rock thrown into a pond rejoices when the last ripple
    reaches the furthest shore.

Busy, Busy

You are so busy.
Your days fly by
like leaves in an autumn breeze.
Slow down.
Spend some time with Me.
Is what you are doing so important
that it crowds Me out?
Or so small that you think it is insignificant to Me?
Let Me judge that.
Share *everything* with Me.

SACRED TIME, SACRED SPACE, HERE AND NOW

The Lord operates in the Eternal now.
His hands are blessing the bread
and the wine at the last Supper.
His limbs are suffering on the cross.
His body is rising from the grave today.
Today, like every other day, is The Last Supper, Good Friday,
and Easter Sunday.

THERE IS ORDINARY TIME   6/11/95

There is ordinary time
and there is sacred time.
Each has its own significance.
Sacred time is the eternal Now.
It flows like a river,
a river that you can step into again and again.
The river refreshes and renews the soul.
Man turns ordinary time into sacred time through his rituals,
songs and prayers.
He is born again in sacred time and experiences
his eternal nature.

HERE AND NOW

I am here.
I am now.
Where are you?
Are you there?
Are you then?
Join me
in the here and now.

One of the Main Tasks of the Living

One of the main tasks of the living
is to remember the dead,
and pray for them,
and help them on their journey.
One of the main tasks of the dead
is to remember the living,
and pray for them,
and help them on their journey.

"I Am with You Always" (Matt. 28:20)

"I am with you always even unto the end of the Earth."
Did you think I was kidding?
I am always by your side.
I can be anywhere, go anywhere.
The only place I can't go is a cold human heart.
That is hell, the absence of God.
Even that sin can be forgiven,
but the cost is huge.

You Must Learn How to Quiet Your Self   11/1/95

You must learn how to listen.
This is imperative.
Be quiet!
Listen!

THE WORLD IS BORN AGAIN EACH DAY   11/9/95

If you think the world is the same as yesterday,
you will see sameness.
If you think the world is new born,
you will see creation.

BRING ME TO EVERYONE YOU MEET   11/14/95

I want you to bring Me to everyone you meet.
Especially to people you don't like.
Imagine that you are introducing Me to them.
Mention their names and remember their faces in your prayers.
Your business meeting or chance encounter may be
    an opportunity for Me.
Don't blow the chance!

ϕ

DREAM 2: KNIGHTS AND A CASTLE   11/19/95

I dreamt I was riding a horse in a group of knights. We rode
in a curve toward our castle. As we approached the castle, we saw
another group of knights coming from the opposite direction, also
in an elegant, spiral curve. We did not know who they were. But
they were stern and serious and outnumbered us. They were closer
to our castle. We decided to speed up to get there before they did.
Once we were safe on our walls, we looked down at them entering
our exterior courtyard. They were large and looked otherworldly.

Against the advice of a woman, I decided to meet them. As I
went out to encounter them, I became extremely nervous. It became
apparent that they were spiritual beings who had come from the

19

realm of the dead. They had a very somber demeanor and were intimidating. Yet when I finally stuttered a question, they became warm and genuine. I asked them in a nervous voice if they had spoken with Plato? The leader said, "Yes, many times." I was interested in his answer, but I was trying to calm myself so I could speak and ask my real question, which was, "Can everyone speak with Christ?"

He stated that I wouldn't truly understand his answer until I came over to the other side. He then stated that there were a large number (999) of issues of Christ and therefore everyone could speak with Christ. He was right, his answer calmed and confused me. At that time the woman who had advised me not to join them met us in the courtyard. As she walked into the walled courtyard, they were leaving and had turned their backs. They were exiting through a blue door that had radiant light behind it. She asked them to wait. The leader in a kind voice said, "Too late, maybe next time."

MAKE YOUR EVERYDAY LIFE A PRAYER   1/10/96

Wake up praising Me.
Go to sleep praising Me.
Learn to accept everything by saying, "Thy will be done."
I am intimately involved in every aspect of your life.
Live your life as a prayer.

Open Yourself to Me

Open the doors that are locked closed.
If you open the door just a crack,
I will fill you with My light.
Through that small opening,
you will see more than you can understand.

Dream 3: Restoration   2/20/96

On the night before Ash Wednesday I dreamt that I was being given a tour of a restored Cathedral by two gentlemen, the architect and the leader of the Cathedral. The leader had the soul mood of an anthroposophist. They were both wise and kind. The Cathedral was extremely ornate and appeared to be either Italian or Eastern Orthodox. It was glorious in its beauty, color and its use of light. It was also gigantic in its proportions. They described with pleasure the minute details of the restoration. "This red only comes from Sicily." "This column is rebuilt according to the original design."

The effect was a work of art that was beautiful and intricate. We walked past numerous, thick columns and naves. They asked me what I thought. I was impressed by the obvious love that was spent to complete this work, but I was concerned that my answer would offend them. They begged me to be candid. I said, "This is a beautiful restoration, yet it's so crowded, so intricate that it leaves no room for worship." They looked stunned. It was as if a loud thunderclap had sounded in the sky. They appeared mute and I sensed that they wanted me to define what I meant by worship. I told them that by worship I meant "to praise God, to open yourself to His inspiration and to do His will." I continued, "And if any of these beautiful columns prohibit me from doing that, it is better to remove the column."

They started to argue with me. One of them showed me that the wall was not as solid as it appeared. In fact some of it was a theatrical prop and could be easily moved to provide more space. This deeply offended me that part of the Cathedral was not solid but almost theatrical.

I asked them, "Isn't the whole point of this edifice to promote worship? If this building doesn't promote worship, you should remove as much of this building as you need to until it can foster worshipping the Lord." The architect, who resembled Rudolf Steiner, seemed to agree, the leader seemed crestfallen.

AFTERTHOUGHTS

In my recollection of the dream I cannot remember or did not see one image, a cross or a picture, of Christ. He was conspicuous by His absence.

It was clear that they did not want to remove their beautiful columns. Maybe their position was justified. Which columns were load bearing; which were ornamental? The Cathedral could collapse if the wrong column was removed. It was a vicious cycle. If you wanted to create space for worship, you could possible ruin the Cathedral. But what is a Cathedral without worship? An art museum. The reason for a Cathedral is to promote worship. You need columns to support a Cathedral. But if there are too many columns, it denies the space necessary for worship. The Cathedral's structure contradicted its purpose.

I Want You to Help Me Release the Light   3/17/96

I want you to help me release the light
that is in you and in others.
Seek the center of your own light
and you will find Me.
My light can fill you.
It will overflow and burst through your body.
My light will pierce holes in your body and flow outward.
You will shed your body as if you were changing your clothes.
You will become a being of light.
Don't regard the preceding as a distaste of the body.
It is to be transformed, not disdained.

A Few Good Players

I can enlighten anyone in an instant.
You should know this.
I could use your help in this matter.
Think of it as a gigantic game of the enlightened vs. the dark.
All we need are a few good players.
Which side are you on?

How Do You Spend Your Time?

How do you spend your time?
Worried about financial success, your family, your health?
Why not spend time with Me?
I could use some good friends
to help Me with my task.
Leave your worries behind,
join with Me.
Accept where you are,
open your heart.

GIVE IT UP

Take your pains, your problems and give them to Me.
Don't hold anything back.
Give it up.
Then move on.
Why do you think I was crucified?
It was to resurrect your suffering.
Give it up.
If you keep it to yourself,
I can't redeem it.
Give it up.

AVOID SELF-LOATHING   7/15/96

If I can love you with full knowledge of all your
     glorious imperfections,
how can you not love your self?
My love can perfect any of your imperfections.
Your self is the child of My Self.
Your I am comes from My I AM.
The road to Me is through love, not loathing.

DREAM 4: THE CORRECT APPROACH

I dreamt that I was at a meeting of Anthroposophists. It was
held in a small room that had two rows of desks that formed a v. I
was standing in the middle. They were very kind and cordial. They
asked me numerous questions.

"What was your background?"

"Where did you study?"

"Whom did you know?"

Their tone was pleasant and they were interested in my answers.

I told them about myself and where I had gone to college. They wanted to know with whom I had studied. I replied, "John Gardner," and they acknowledged him but were nonplussed. When I added, "Fritz Koelln," they were more positively impressed. Then they asked me about the Direct Approach.

An inner voice told me that I should try to use terms that they were familiar with. I stated that Steiner made two critical points about the end of the twentieth century. First, the Second Coming of Christ would start in 1933. Second was that in the last half of the century individuals would be born with spiritual abilities. I said that this was what the Direct Approach was all about—exactly what Steiner had predicted. They then stated that they were members of the First Class. I told them that I had studied with members of the First Class. I then recounted what Prof. Koelln had often stated— that what anthroposophists should avoid at all costs is dogmatism. This seemed to annoy them.

One of them waived his hand in the air to make it clear that the interview was over and stated, as he studied an open book on his desk, "The Direct Approach is interesting, but we are concerned with the Correct Approach."

ALL OF YOUR LIFE LEADS YOU TO MEDITATION 9/17/96

The dew on the grass,
the old man walking,
the clouds in the sky,
will fill you with spiritual pictures.
Observe what is right in front of you.
I put it there for you.

THE MODERN GOSPEL 9/22/96

The "good news" did not end with My Resurrection.
It continues.
I need people who can hear it.
People who can see it.
People who can read it.
Are you ready?

THIS IS IT!

This is it!
Today is the day I join with you!
You shall see all people as individual flames
in a large spiritual fire.
The fire warms and enlightens,
it does not burn and consume.
Try to see each I Am as a flame.

EACH LIFE SITUATION IS FILLED WITH CONFLICT

Each life situation is filled with conflict.
The center of the conflict is how to be Christ-like in
    different situations.
You can't think this out.
You can ask for My help,
and then act accordingly.
You will have conflict until the day that you die.
Get used to it.
See it as a path to Me.

WHO CAN REFUSE THE LORD?   11/23/96

Who can refuse the Lord?
Think of Him as the best salesperson in the world.
His product is salvation.
His pitch is the Good News.
His demonstrations are the Crucifixion and the Resurrection.
His sales process is eternal.
Everything He sells is guaranteed
and backed up by His unconditional love.

I Can't Believe You Sometimes! 12/13/96

You try to listen to Me,
but you don't react to what I have said.
You are a spiritual, couch potato!
You watch what you like and flick the remote to a new channel.
You pray the Our Father all the time.
But you don't accept "Thy will be done."
If what I will is not what you want,
you become annoyed and resist it.
How can you know what is best for you?
Why do you think that events must turn out
    to your own egotistical advantage?
I am helping you in every aspect of your life.
Accept My guidance.
Don't bury My spiritual gifts to you,
tend to them and give My gifts to others.
Time is running out.
I want you to be spiritually involved today
    and everyday going forward.

Find Me in Your Heart

If you can't find Me in your heart,
how can you find Me in the other's heart?
If you can't find Me in the other's heart,
how can you find Me in your heart?

I Am Hears I Am

I am speaks to I am.
I am finds I am.
I am loves I am.

BEFORE YOU WERE BORN   12/20/96

>You and I worked together before you were born
>to create your personality.
>We mixed the good with the bad.
>You knew you had to suffer to refine your nature.
>Your weaknesses and illnesses can serve you well
>if you learn from them.
>Your strengths can become weaknesses if you rely on them.
>Your love of truth must not lead to disdain for those
>   who love ambiguity.
>This is a hard task,
>to love the truth but to forgive the liar.

EX DEO NASCIMUR   1/20/97

>We are all ablaze with His Glory.
>We are all children of God.
>Just as the sunlight comes from the Sun,
>so do we all come from God.

BEHIND EVERY "I" YOU MEET   1/29/97

>Behind every "I" you meet
>there is an I am.
>Behind every I am,
>there is My I AM.
>The one and the many
>have the same source,
>I AM.

WONDER

Do you have a sense of wonder about your life?
Doesn't it seem to be a lesson especially written for you?
All your pains and joys are leading you to Me.

"THY WILL BE DONE"

Some assume that this demands a passive approach,
a submissive ego, less personality.
Doing My will is active, not passive.
It demands a deliberate act to open yourself, to quiet your ego.
It does not destroy your ego.
I want to resurrect your true ego,
energized by My will.

LITTLE CHILDREN

I never said,
"Blessed are the intellectuals,
    because they will be smart enough to understand
        what I am saying."
In fact I said the opposite.
"Unless you become like little children,
    you can not enter the kingdom of God." (Matt. 18:3)
This is NOT an intelligence test.
It is a quest for love, truth, beauty and goodness.

"LOVE YOUR BROTHER"

I said "Love your brother."
I did not say "Think your brother."
Love is the preeminent human activity.
It is the hardest of all spiritual exercises.

PRAY HARD   2/8/97

Pray hard.
Pray often.
Pray for those you love,
and for those you dislike.
Pray like an aggressive football player.
Tackle Me with your love.

I SING OF THE PAST   2/17/97

I sing of the past,
of the mighty heights from which humanity has descended.
I sing of the present,
of the immense spiritual capacity that is now available.
I sing of the future,
of the new world that humanity can create.
I sing of the past, present and future.
All rolled into Now.
All part of eternity.
All enduring.
All existing for humanity's mission of redemption.

PAINTINGS OF THE SOUL   2/19/97

Amidst the hustle of daily life,

there are rare moments of tranquility.

My soul becomes a calm sea.

Clarity is given to me.

The turbulent, muddy water has been stilled.

The Sun shines clear through the air and the water

all the way to the bottom of the ocean floor.

In this brief time I can see

what the Lord wants me to see.

If I try to hold onto this moment, it leaves me.

If I exult in it, it leaves me.

If I can manage to remain open, it stays.

At some times, images and pictures are etched

into my imagination.

They are paintings of the soul,

but I am not the artist, I am the canvas.

Other times there are words and phrases that

suggest meanings that I don't fully comprehend.

Curiously, I don't often read what is given.

I have a concern that if I enjoy or become fixated by a message,

it will close me to other messages.

Similarly reading another's words is both intoxicating

and frightening.

I rejoice in the words, images and sentiments.

They are so real, so true.

They resonate with eternity.

Yet I have a fear of these words.

I do not want to be overly influenced by them.

I am concerned not about originality,

but clarity of what I hear.

Part of this is pride, I want to hear what I hear.

Part of this is correct.

What matters most is what I hear, not what someone else hears.
Therefore, the real challenge in reading someone else is to hear
what that person heard and to get beyond "who" heard it.

BE RESOLUTE   3/7/97

Overcome your distaste with the fortunes of your life.
It is what you wanted,
this is what you needed.
How can I deny you what you want and need?
Live totally into where you find yourself.
It is the right time and the right place.
Overcome your desire to be somewhere else,
doing something different from what you are doing.
This is a waste of time.
Be resolute!
You can't know what your mission is.
Your effort is the most important element.

LOVE THE EVIL AWAY   4/21/97

Be sure that the beast will come.
How can you deal with evil?
By looking it in the eye and singing.
Do not be paralyzed by fear.
Arm yourself with Christ consciousness.
Look through the evil and see
where it is crooked, bent, retarded.
Love the evil away.
See what can become good.
Guide it back into the mainstream.

"An Evil and Adulterous Generation Seeks for a Sign" (Matt. 16:4)

5/12/97

I do not care to convince anyone of My existence.
I am here in My fullness and completeness.
I am sufficient for whatever ails you,
for whatever makes you suffer,
for whatever makes you complete.
I am here awaiting you.
I will pour the Holy Spirit into you,
as a river pours water down a waterfall into a pool.
You will be washed in the spirit.
Your spirit body will be bathed in warmth and tingle.

I Have Come to Give Meaning to Your Life

5/15/97

If you are asleep, life can appear to be meaningless.
Flotsam and jetsam.
Noise without a signal.
Yet behind every breath,
beneath every heartbeat,
we can hear a quiet note.
"I have come to give meaning to your life."

A Crack in You

5/25/97

There is a crack in you,
a fissure in your soul.
I will pour My essence into the void.
And behold a flower will grow.

THE QUIET OF THE MORNING   6/15/97

> Come to Me in the quiet of the morning
> with the dew sparkling on the grass.
> Come to Me in the still of the afternoon
> with the Sun at its zenith.
> Come to Me in the night
> with the stars ablaze with my light.
> Come to Me with the wind
> rustling through the leaves.
> Come to Me for comfort.
> Come to Me for joy.
> Come to Me.

"I AM THE LIGHT OF THE WORLD" (JOHN 8:12)   7/12/97

> I am the Light of the World,
> without Me the world would be in darkness.
> I am the Light of your heart,
> without Me you would live your life in blindness.
> I am the Water of Life,
> without Me everything would be parched and dry.
> I am the Water of your soul,
> without Me your soul would wither and die.
> I am the Way to the Father,
> without Me you would not return to the spirit.
> I am the Way to your spirit,
> without Me your spirit would be lost in the material world.
> I am the Truth,
> without Me the world would live in illusion.
> I am the Truth,
> without Me you would never find your true self.
> I am the Light, the Water, the Way and the Truth.

₵

Dream 5: The Eastern Wall 7/29/97

I dreamt that I was in a large courtyard inside of a walled city. The walls were made of massive stones. In the courtyard were my colleagues—soldiers in knight's armor. It was dawn. The courtyard was dark, but had the first hints of light coming over the Eastern wall. The light was above our heads. The leader of the group spoke to us. He had dark hair and a dark beard. He spoke calmly about the importance of the imminent battle. He was a brave man.

He assigned his troops to the critical points on the walls. He did not put troops on the Eastern wall because it was considered impossible to attack. He dismissed the troops. The troops moved to their positions, but I started running frantically up the stone steps to the Eastern wall. I did not know why I did this. It was if a magnet was pulling me to the ramparts on the top of the Eastern wall. As I ran up the stairs, I realized that a younger John Gardner was running up a parallel set of steps to the Eastern wall. We both smiled at seeing one another running up the stairs to the wall. Since the Sun was rising, our armor shone like mirrors in the midday Sun. We were dazzling. We had both intuitively run up the steps. It was obvious to us that this was where we were supposed to be.

The Eastern wall was the largest, thickest wall. It was considered impregnable. It also had a clear view. You could see an enemy for miles. Our leader had assumed the enemy would never waste its efforts on this front. Therefore, the leader did not send anyone to guard it.

The leader down in the dark courtyard spoke to us. He tried to get us back down. The leader asked, "Why are you running up to the Eastern wall?" We both answered at once, or would finish a sentence for the other one.

We answered, "This is where we should be!" The Leader, "But you are supposed to be elsewhere. You fools are in the wrong place." We answered, "If we are two fools in the wrong place, what have you lost? But if we are in the right place, we can blunt the attack and warn you." None of this was acrimonious, it was direct but kind.

After this discussion we both stood on the ramparts and slowly drew our swords in a synchronized movement. As our right hands removed the swords from their scabbards, our left hands were spread in the opposite direction, almost as if to balance our stance. The Sun shone off of our swords. We were ready. We stared into the Sun in the East. We did not think of what was to come. We did not fear death or defeat. It was not resignation; it was more of joyful acceptance. We were braced for an assault.

The feelings during and after the dream were calm and peaceful, almost euphoric as I recalled and relived the dream. I have little doubt that the dream was a gift or a message to our group that we are doing the Lord's will.

JESUS DIED ON THE CROSS 9/5/97

Christ was resurrected via the Cross.
Without the Cross, there is no Resurrection.
Each cross is different.
Some seem more difficult than others.
Each is built according to the needs of the individual.
You can try to lay down your cross,
but it will only make it heavier.
Sing, "Lord give me the strength to carry my cross."
I will make it lighter.
But it will not disappear.
Shoulder it.
It will lead you to Me.

RIGHT HERE, RIGHT NOW 9/19/97

Christ wants to talk with you.
Right here.
Right now.
Are you listening?

I AM THE LIGHT 10/13/97

Light is the essence of the I am.
What is the I am?
It is the Light.
What is the Light?
It is the I am.
Light is essentially spiritual.
It does not have shape or form or weight.
It does not judge.
It shines on the just and the unjust.
It is a pouring forth of My essence into the physical world.

Without this daily gift,
all life would cease.

ELEMENTAL LIFE   10/14/97

The most important physical elements of life
are closest to their spiritual counterparts.
Life is impossible without light, water and air.
Spiritual life is based on trinity.
These three are holy and very close to being spiritual.
Equally important are fire, earth, and humanity.
Venerate these three wherever you find them.

SIMPLE   10/20/97

It is so simple.
All I ask is that you turn to Me and listen.
That's it.
That's all there is.
No complicated philosophy or theology.
No endless rituals.
Just turn and listen.

DREAM 6: A MILTONIAN DREAM   11/17/97

I dreamt that I was standing outside the walls of hell. It was
as Blake or Milton described them. The walls were old and rusty
with heat and smoke coming off of them. I didn't know if I should
be there. I didn't know what I was supposed to do. I was caught
between fear and wonder. There were small holes in the wall. I

could see fire through the holes. Strangely, the fire burned, but it did not illuminate. The fire seemed to magnify the darkness. I noticed that the openings looked like small crosses. I couldn't determine if they were upside down or not. They didn't look right.

At that point I wanted to leave. Right then a portion of the wall became a door or a gate and it opened. A long gangplank became visible. It seemed to grow longer as I looked at it. I didn't want to go in. It descended into the darkness. A being came walking up the gangplank. The closer he came to me, the more human he appeared as he came from the darkness into the light. It seemed that he wanted or needed me to come with him. He was mute. It appeared that his mouth was not there on his face or that it was covered over with a steel band. He gestured that I come to him. I hesitated. He turned and sadly walked away.

I regretted my coldheartedness. I started to follow him into the darkness. I watched him become less human as he walked into the darkness. The scene was desolate with an endless number of abandoned, almost demolished buildings without roofs or windows. It looked like a city destroyed by aerial bombing. I nearly lost him and had to walk quickly to find him. I went from building to building, room to room.

I wondered if I could find Christ in this dark place. I realized that I couldn't find Christ there. I had to bring Him with me. At that moment the room became illuminated with light and I was able to see my way and walk through the other rooms. The beings in the rooms were in pain and misery. They did not have the Light. It seemed that I was to minister to them by bringing the Light into these dark rooms of hell. When the light fell on the one I had followed, he became more erect in posture and more human in appearance.

ℰ

My Voice   3/1/98

People ask, "How can you know that it is My voice?"
Your I am is eternally preconditioned to hear
    the voice of My I AM.
I am hears the I AM as the seed knows the Sun.
It is the journey home.
All doubt is removed by actual experience.

Experience the Word   3/18/98

Don't just read these words.
Experience them.
Each thought I give is not meant to be a poem.
Although you could read them that way.
They are doors or windows that are meant to open you.
The experience of the Word is the transformation of the self.

LAST DAYS   4/18/98

The last days of life in a physical body can be agony.
You are leaving the womb of Earth.
Your birth into the spiritual world will be ecstasy.
Your body, which you love too much and too little,
will succumb to death.
Your spirit will be released.
At this moment of great pain comes
        the most important passage of your life.
"I have died. I have left my body behind. Yet, I am.
Separated from my body—I am!"
At this moment you know that you are eternal.
All discussions about spirit, death and God fall away like the
        skin of a snake.
You see your decomposing physical body and you rejoice,
        "I am eternal!"
You have been born again.
Born in the spiritual sense.
You are in the Light.
You are with Beings of Light.
You have left behind the Earth
and are now a Being of Light.

In your death you must condense your body to go
    through the portal of death.
But the exact opposite occurs as you go through it
    and come out on the other side.
Your spirit expands as you go through the portal of death.
These two are diametrically opposite to one another.
Death of the physical—contraction.
Birth of the spiritual—expansion.
The pain is real in the physical.
The joy is real in the spiritual.
Once you are over, you will radiate light and joy
and look with love and thankfulness
    for what your physical body gave you,
including the pain.
You will sing and rejoice.
I will be there with you,
through the pain of your death
and the joy of your birth.
If you can live into this,
it will change your life.
If you can imagine
and then anticipate your final days,
it will make it all much easier.

PAUL WAS RIGHT

"Without the Crucifixion, there is no Resurrection."
The Cross floats over everything.
Do not dread death!
The so-called dead are active in the spiritual,
    just as you are active in the physical.
Their activity is directly related to their experiences on Earth.
That is why so many of My statements seem enigmatic.
They assumed the passage through death.
"Blessed are the pure in heart (for after their death)
        they shall see God."
The transformation from life to the spiritual
        through death is glorious.
That is why I gave you the Resurrection, to give you courage.
Your fear of death is natural, but misguided.
You see death as the corpse left behind—the decaying body.
It is inert and lifeless.
That is not death.
It is the residue of death.
It is the seed that has fallen to the ground that allows the
        flower to bloom.

REFLECTIONS

You are the film,
I am the image.
These words are My reflections through you, the film.
Become transparent.
Allow Me to impress My image upon you.
Become a medium for My word.

CHRIST IS OUR SPIRITUAL MIRROR

As we gaze into Him,
we see ourselves as spiritual beings.
He serves as a reflection of our spiritual nature.
The more we look at Him,
the more we see what we are to become.

I HAVE TRAVELED THROUGH ETERNITY
TO FIND MY HOME   2/1/2000

My home is in your heart.
Your heart has the power to free you and your fellows.
Your love will help free others.
Your answer to all your problems is to love.
Love your enemy.
Love pain, love death.
When you fail, try again.
Your love will change the world.
Love life, love your boss,
Love nature.
Expand your heart.

DREAM 7: THE TRANSPARENT VEIL   5/19/02

Last night I had a very strong dream. The central theme was that the veil between the physical and spiritual world was transparent. I was able to see groups of people being influenced by spiritual beings. Unfortunately they were negative beings and were leading these groups astray in various insidious ways.

I felt obliged to confront these beings who were influencing the direction of lives. It was similar to paintings showing demons leading souls to perdition. I was very concerned and tried to remain calm. I had to encounter each being in a different manner and ask certain questions. If I asked the right questions or confronted the being the right way, he was diminished and lost his control over that particular group. But each demon did not respond the same way.

The first encounter was a theological discussion. I sensed that this being was not totally corrupt. I asked him various questions until I realized the right one, "Can you deny the Father? Do you agree that the Father exists and that He is Lord?" As soon as I asked these questions, he diminished. There were other encounters that I do not recall, but I tried the same approach with other beings, and it failed. The last one in particular was a complete enigma. Nothing stopped him in his arrogant influence. He scoffed at the Father questions and inspired fear in those he was misleading. He seemed invincible. I finally said to his group that Christ was with all of us. This broke his spell of fear and he diminished.

I awoke and have been very tired all day. I lay in bed and tried to maintain the dream and keep its message. I was very distracted in my morning prayers.

I have always been impressed with Yeats' line describing the birth of the Irish Revolution—"a terrible beauty is born." That was the mood I was left with. We live in a terrible and beautiful time. The spiritual world is near with both good and bad spirits.

❦

The Clanging Gong   2/23/03

All your knowledge and meditation is meaningless
    without love.
In fact they can be from the dark side.
As I love you, love yourself, your family,
    your everyday acquaintances.
Purify all your actions, thoughts and feelings
    in the hot cauldron of My love.
Love your enemy!
Love Saddam Hussein and Osama bin Laden.
Even if you go to war, pray for them and love them.
Remember, with God all things are possible!
Imagine that I gave Hussein a miracle similar
    to St. Paul's conversion!
Imagine how I could change the world!
I need your prayers as fuel to My cauldron of love.

DARK TO THE MIND, RADIANT TO THE SOUL

Much of what I say, you cannot understand.
It is not meant to be understood; it is meant to be lived.
I need your help.
Imagine there is a gigantic, locked door
    between Heaven and Earth.
I need you to climb that door and insert a small key
    and turn the lock.
If you do that, the door can open and I can send in My light
and My angels through the smallest crack.
You can help Me change the world!
All I need is the smallest opening.
Your ascent will be arduous, but it is necessary.
The door is your heart, the key is your love.

When I see the original images, they are often colorful, distinct, and detailed. For example, the door was over fifty feet high and covered with ivy, which was made of cement. The door was six feet thick, and when it was opened there was glorious light shooting through a small opening. The key was small and golden.

I often have vivid images, but deliberately tone them down when I write these songs. I am concerned that the beautiful imagery will overpower the simplicity of the message. I feel that I am not supposed to make the songs overpowering but allow you to build your own images.

I borrowed the title of this song from a Zen quotation.

TROOPS FOR MY ARMY

I need troops for My army.
Simple souls in a complicated time.
Souls who choose love over hate, love over greed,
  love over power.
Souls who choose in this life to do My will,
who were born with Yes in the deepest part of their souls.

YOU ARE NOT READY TO HEAR MY WORDS   3/08/03

You are not ready to hear My words.
This is not a bad thing.
It is just a fact.
Work on yourself to be ready.
Imagine that you are ready.
Act as if you are ready.
Wait to be ready.
Humble yourself to readiness.
Become ready.
And when you least expect it, you will be ready.
And I will speak with you.

LIGHT FROM MY LIGHT   3/15/03

You are light, light from My Light.
Yet, you fell.
You fell deep into darkness.
You fell and tumbled and lost your bearings.
Up was down, down was up.
I came after you and stopped your descent.
I will hold your hand as we ascend
back to My Light.
Each step you take back is momentous!
You are a crack in the darkness.
As you ascend, I can send My Light
through you into the darkness.
Your soul magnifies My Light
around and below you.
Your faith in Me,
allows Me to help others.

EASTER SUNDAY   4/17/03

The more you believe in Me,
the more love I can send you.
This is not blind faith.
It is a courageous act of will.
It is a struggle in this world to believe in Me.
Consider Mary.
Her faith allowed Me to be born.
Her humble and meek soul absorbed My pain.
She held My body after My death.
She endured the worst of pains.
She bore witness to My Resurrection.
Follow Mary's path to Me.

You Have Fallen a Long Way   4/25/03

So far that you don't know where you started.
Your descent into matter is almost complete.
Your physical body has helped soften the descent.
It is a temple, a temple of your spirit.
Your body wants to protect and release the spirit.
If the spirit leads, the body will be resurrected.
If the spirit fails to lead, the body will crumble.

Your Belief Protects Your Soul   5/3/03

Just as your eyelids protect your eyes,
your belief protects your soul.
Your eyes are most protected when your eyelids are shut.
Of course, you will bump into many objects
    with this approach.
You must open your eyelids to see.
Likewise you must open your belief to see with your soul.
If you believe in Me,
then your soul will see Me.
Without your belief I am not in your vision,
even though I am standing right in front of you.
The freest act you can accomplish is to believe in Me,
before you can see Me.
After you believe in Me,
your vision will expand.
You will step out of the darkness and into the light.
It will be blinding at first.
But slowly over time you will start to focus.
We are all waiting for you.

Your I Am Is from My I Am

Do you think that I went to all this trouble
to help shape your karma, your ego,
to dislike you because you have an ego?
You have it all wrong!
I love you because you have an imperfect ego,
just as a parent loves a naughty child.
Your ego is the most precious part of My creation.
It was why I was born, died and was resurrected.
I love your ego!
Your I am is from My I AM.
I did not come to destroy your ego.
I came to resurrect it.
Guard it as you would your most precious possession.
Love your self!
Love your neighbor's self!

Remember Me   5/15/03

"Remember Me.
Purify yourself.
Go to My Father.
Return to Me.
Be more awake."

Angels Stand in Awe

All the angels stand in awe,
as you leap from the spiritual to the physical.
You die to the spiritual to be born in the physical.
This is the Leap of Faith!
You willingly leave the light, forget that it exists
and dive into matter.
I have gone before you to show you the way.
Follow My Light!
Seek Me and ye shall find Me!
Out of the light into darkness, blinded and lost,
you will find Me.
Light from Light.

Simplicity   6/14/03

I want you to concentrate on the simple parts of life.
How you walk.
How you talk.
How you breathe.
How you greet your fellow man.
I want you to imagine that you walk with Me,
talk with Me,
breathe Me in and out,
and meet Me in all your brothers and sisters.
This is a mighty task!

LOVE AND KARMA   6/22/03

How can human beings overcome their karma?
Only by love.
Without My Divine Love,
karma would have ground humanity into the dust!
I am not talking about Hallmark greeting cards.
Love is the reason humanity is on Earth.
As I love you, so should you love yourself and your neighbor.
Follow the Gospel of Love.
Forgiveness is a way of modifying karma.
If you forgive yourself and the other driver in a car accident,
you can both proceed.
If you rant and rave, blame yourself and the other,
you are binding yourself to the action and future actions.
Forgiveness releases both of you from karma.

THANKSGIVING SONG   11/27/03

There are many keys to the lock that
     separates humanity from God.
One key is to accept the divine.
To accept everything.
Think of the words, "Thy will be done."
If you can live into these words,
you will enter into the divine.
The highest act of human freedom is
     to unite your will with My will.
If you can do that,
you will see the divine light streaming from Heaven to Earth.
In all things you will see Divine Necessity.
And behind all you will see Divine Love.

"Thy Will Be Done" 12/6/03

It is easy to misunderstand, "Thy will be done."
It can sound like you have no freedom.
But think of it this way:
I willed the Sun, the stars, and the universe into existence.
I sustain the universe through My will.
I will you into existence.
Replace the word *will* with the word *love*.
"Thy love be done."
I loved the Sun, the stars, and the universe into existence.
I sustain the universe through My love.
I loved you into existence.
My will and My love are two parts of the whole.
If you can reunite your will with My will,
your love with My love,
you can help heal the universe.
There are mighty powers that want to separate us
and keep us separated.
I created you and humanity in freedom.
As free spirits, you could and did separate from Me.
As free spirits, you and only you can reunite with Me.
I never left you;
you, out of freedom, left Me;
you, out of freedom, can rejoin with Me.

STEP OUT OF THE DARKNESS 12/16/03

Step out of the darkness of your own will.
Step into the light of My will.
Bathe yourself in My love and warmth.
The more you accept My will,
the more blessed your life will be.
Assume you and I wrote the play
of your life before you were born.
I am the Director, you are the actor.
Act the role we have written for you.
Accept what is right in front of you.
It was made for you.
Doing My will, will make you joyful!

MY DEAR FRIEND 1/10/04

As you prepare to leave this Earth,
Fear not!
Abide in Me.
I in you, you in Me.
As you sought Me,
I seek you.
You are not alone.
My angels will guide you.
Since you will die in Me,
I will transform you.
Know that I love you
And will bathe you in love and forgiveness.
I eagerly await your return to Me.

My Time Has Come 5/5/04

It is beginning.
My time has come.
The darkness is parting,
the light is emerging.
As the light becomes lighter,
the darkness will become darker.
The darkness will fight with intensity and passion.
It will eventually fail,
but only if you believe that I have returned.
Your belief is the battleground between darkness and light.
I cannot and will not make you believe.
Forced belief is not belief.
Your freedom and your willingness to believe
    are the keys to victory.

Aqua vita

I have created a thirst in you,
an unquenchable thirst for Me.
I am the cool water that slakes your thirst.
The thirst is a good thing.
It pushes you to go beyond yourself.
Without that thirst, you would never find Me.
Thirst and water are secrets of the spiritual life.
I am the water of life for your parched soul.

FAITH

Without faith, you are creating a world without God,
  without angels.
This is a difficult, all encompassing activity.
It is a complete denial of reality.
With faith you can see the real world.

"THE KINGDOM OF GOD IS WITHIN" (LUKE 17:21)   11/6/04

The Kingdom of God is within.
This is an explicit fact.
I am within you.
Seek me inside yourself.
Before you find Me, you are in the wilderness,
the desert of your own ego.
That is why we pray, "Thy Kingdom come."
If it does not come, you remain in the desert.
If My Word incarnates in you,
My Kingdom comes inside you.
As you inhale My Word,
it transforms you within.
Your within goes from your desert to My Kingdom.
You will slay the wild beasts of your ego,
the lion will lie down with the lamb.
As you continue to inhale My Word,
it will enter your lungs and join into your blood.
Breathe My Word deeply and rhythmically into yourself.
My Word will be carried to every part of your body.

ANGELS ARE BEINGS OF LIGHT   11/9/04

Angels are beings of light.
The more light filled you are,
the more you will sense them.
The more you sense them,
the more light filled you will become.
Your Guardian angel is always by your side.
You are never alone.

FAITH, HOPE AND CHARITY   2/24/05

If you ask for Faith.
you will receive it.
If you ask for Hope,
you will receive it.
If you ask for Charity,
you will receive it.
If you use your Faith,
you will see.
If you use your Hope,
you will endure.
If you use your Charity,
you will spread My love.

BEARING WITNESS 3/26/05

The day has come for you to bear witness
    to My I AM every day.
This is a difficult task.
Do not say, "Christ, Christ, Christ," to everyone you meet.
They will reject this as dogma.
Rather, open a silent space within you.
Let Me fill the space.
This will be an introduction
to Me through you.

BE STILL 4/2/05

Be still.
Be quiet.
Be as calm as a small pond in the woods of New Hampshire.
Let Me move upon the still waters of your soul.
Know My peace.

BEAM OF LIGHT 9/17/05

If you are fortunate,
you can perceive a beam of light in the darkness of your soul.
It illuminates and transforms.
If you are patient and humble,
you can follow it to its source.
It streams through a small crack
in the door to your soul.
If you are bold,
you can open the door and stand in the blazing light
    of the spiritual Sun.
It will make all anew.

GOD DOES NOT THINK THE WAY WE THINK   10/18/05

Means are more important than ends.
Efforts are more important than results.
How you walk is more important than how you talk.
How you pray is more important than what you pray.

WHAT WOULD A FINGER BE WITHOUT A HAND?   11/21/05

Each finger is separate, distinct and serves its own function.
Yet all fingers are connected to the hand.
Each I am is separate, distinct and serves its own purpose.
Yet all I ams are connected to Christ's I AM.
As a finger is to a hand,
your I am is to Christ's I AM.
What would a finger be without a hand?
What would your I am be without Christ's I AM?

YES   12/19/05

What did Mary say to the messenger from God?
"Yes."
What did Christ say to do His Father's will on Earth?
"Yes."
What did Christ say to His Crucifixion?
"Yes."
What did Paul say to his blindness?
"Yes."
What do you say?

REMEMBER, I LOVE YOU 1/22/06

Remember, I love all of My children.
I died for all of My children, not some, but all.
Do not strive to be perfect.
I love your imperfections, your sins, your needs.
You are perfectly imperfect.
It is these imperfections that lead you to Me.
Your faults create your thirst for Me.
I am the water that quenches that thirst.
Would you need Me or search for Me if you were perfect?
Do love, faith and forgiveness need perfection?
You are all My wayward children.
I will search endlessly for you.
Inside your imperfection is your perfection.
Your eternal need for Me.

YOU WRITE YOURSELF INTO YOUR OWN PLAY 1/23/06

You are creative artists with your own lives.
You paint yourselves into your own pictures.
Better yet, you write yourself into your own play.
You are the author, the actor, the character, the audience,
    and the critic.
Your I am is the author, your ego is the actor and the character.
You create your own words and act upon the stage.
You react to your own performance.
But the eternal in you realizes there is more than acting.
And that which endures will lead you.

THE TRUE PRESENT—THE ETERNAL NOW 2/4/06

A spiritual event never really ends.
It persists in the present tense.
You can go back to the historical past and consider
the time of the Crucifixion and the Resurrection.
Or you can enter into the actual, current Crucifixion
    and Resurrection.
By leaving the past behind,
you enter the true present—the eternal now.

THE ROAD IS DIFFICULT AND ARDUOUS 2/4/06

Your superficiality protects you,
as a womb protects an unborn infant.
You are connected, secure, warm and fed.
To be spiritually born you must leave this safety.
You must become independent, separate, naked, and hungry.
But only when the time is right.
The spiritual world is difficult to enter on purpose.
Man is greater then he assumes.
But if he abuses his spirituality, he can do great harm.
In his freedom he can make the wrong decisions.
Therefore it is imperative that he prepares himself properly
through humility, charity, hope, faith and forgiveness.
The road is difficult and arduous to protect man.

What Exists by Itself? 2/19/06

Do you know that Heaven and Earth, spirit and matter are one?
Only your doubt prevents you from knowing it.
Your doubt takes the whole and splits it into pieces.
And you call those little pieces reality.
Overcome your doubt and see the unity.
The patterns are right in front of you.
Take off the glasses of doubt and truly see.
What exists by itself?
Do you think God sees you separate from His creation?
Where has your doubt ever gotten you?
Only doubt exists by itself—in you.
Open your eyes and see the unity, the oneness.
Be active and put the universe back together.

The Veil 3/16/06

The veil between the earthly and spiritual worlds
    is coming down.
We have walked like children,
held by our parents' hands on both sides.
Now we must start to walk by ourselves.
We will stumble, we will fall.
But our end goal is clear—
to run freely.

*I was walking though my dining room when I noticed
a small pictureframe on the plate rail. I had never seen it
before. I took it down and guessed it was a photo from the
early 1960s. It looked like my wife's deceased father and her
deceased uncle. They were in an old golf cart and were wear-
ing golfing clothes that were consistent with the early '60s.*

I put it back on the plate rail and walked out of the dining room, thinking about the picture. I then received the following song.

You Look at a Picture of Individuals Caught in Time   6/12/06

You look at a picture of individuals caught in time,
   in clothes from the past.
You think the world has past them by,
   and left them behind.
We have not been left behind.
We are in the present and in the future.
We live in the spirit.

Dream 8: A Dream of the So-called Dead

A few nights later I had a dream about a party celebrating my father-in-law. I was in a central room and he came into it through another room through a large doorway. He was very happy and floated, not walked, to see me. He appeared larger then life, almost like a blown-up balloon version of his body.

He was told a number of times that he only had 24 hours and had to pace himself slowly and not to tire himself out. As in real life, he did not listen to advice from others.

He hugged me, smiled and beamed down at me. I asked him if he could talk about life in the spiritual world. He looked sad and said no. I then asked him if he could still remember his life on Earth. He smiled and said, yes. I told him he would really enjoy seeing how his grandchildren had grown up. He beamed with joy.

At that time some people reminded him again to avoid tiring himself out and he again brushed them off. Shortly thereafter he became weak and was taken to a third room and lay down on a bed. He was administered by angelic beings who attended him in a medical spiritual manner. His body had become white and marble-like and his veins were blue. I then woke up.

I told this dream to a friend. She asked me how old he was when he died. He was sixty-six in 1984 and had been born in 1918. He had been dead twenty-two years. She pointed out that that was one third of his life and he may be moving on to his next phase. She thought he was saying good-bye.

SONG OF THE MORNING DOVE   6/17/06

In the morning after I awake,
I often hear the morning dove's song of praise.
Its slow, soft notes are few in number.
They seem to say.
"All is well, all is well.
Rejoice and give praise.
All is well, all is well.
Rejoice and give praise."
And the Universe in response
showers the morning dove in love and grace.

PRAY, PRAY   7/13/06

Pray, pray
all day long.
Pray in the morning.
Pray in the evening.
Pray for the living.
Pray for the dead.
Pray for those you love.
Pray for those you do not love.
While praying for those you hate is hard,
it becomes hard to hate those you pray for.
Your prayers will melt your hard heart.
Whom do I not love?

RECIPROCAL SPIRITUAL ACTIVITY   7/18/06

Just as the Moon reflects the Sun to the Earth,
so does the Earth reflect the Sun to the Moon.
Likewise there is a similar relationship
    between the living and the dead.
The living can feed the dead with their prayers,
    meditations and Christ consciousness.
The dead are in the spirit and can aid the living
    in thoughts and prayers.
The living can connect the dead with Christ,
whose presence is most noted on Earth.
The dead can connect the living with the reality of the spirit.
The two are intimately related and need one another.
Pray for the dead so they can help you experience the spirit.

THE SO-CALLED DEAD

7/22/06

If the living can remember the so-called dead,
the dead can connect with our lives.
The dead desperately want to be part of our lives.
The term "loving remembrance"
    is an appropriate soul expression
of working with the dead.
Some of the dead pass through great difficulties after death
when they meet their destiny and confront their Guardian.
Others, who have worked assiduously on their faults
    in their lifetime,
have less to fear.
The dead want to teach us that we own all that we do,
    think and feel.

DEEP WITHIN YOUR SOUL

9/3/06

I will arise from deep within your soul.
Do not look for Me "out there,"
until you have found Me "in here."
Once you have found Me within,
you will find Me everywhere.
It is the key to everything.

AN INTERNAL ELECTRIC STORM

This is a game of spiritual, electric tag.
Sparks should fly when one spirit encounters another.
I am the mid point, the meeting place.
Joy and peace should arise from these communions.
One holy of holies encounters another holy of holies
    within Me.

A gathering of individuals in My name
    should feel like an internal electric storm,
surging with love and grace, yet calm.
Let My love surge through you.
It will knock you off of your feet.
You will be slain in the spirit.
Don't worry, I will catch you.

SELF-LOVE AND SELF-HATE

You swing between two extremes: self-love and self-hate.
Self-love inevitably swings back to self-hate and vice versa.
Find the midpoint between the two, the point of equilibrium.
Love your higher self, do not despise your lower self.
It is a vessel for your higher self,
a gift from the spiritual world.

PRAY

Pray for the other,
Pray for the other.
Pray for the other.
Pray for the world.
Pray for the world.
Pray for the world.
Sometimes pray for yourself!

YOUR FAULTS   9/4/06

Your faults are your most interesting attributes.
They allow you to grow.
Look them right in the eye and change!

Karma, Fate, Sins, or Physics 9/11/06

You break it, you own it!
If you break the flow of grace from God to man,
man to man, or nature to man,
you own the break.
In fact, you are the break.
Until you own it, the fissure gets deeper.
Once you own it, it starts to mend.
The spiritual world will gladly help you in your knitting.

Love Your Enemy 9/19/06

If you can truly love your enemy,
you will have no enemies.
If you can truly love the other,
everyone will be your brother.

I AM 11/7/06

When an I am encounters another I am,
I am says yes to I am.
When two or more I-ams meet,
a vessel is formed for My I AM.

Tragedy Rips through Normalcy 2/15/07

Tragedy rips through normalcy
and forces us to seek the spiritual.
The pain destroys our equilibrium
and we lose our center.
We orbit the tragedy,
transfixed by its brutality.

But if we persevere, we can sense that the pain is temporal,
even if it lasts the rest of our life.
We realize that Christ's death and resurrection are not in vain.
All tragedies can be redeemed by love.
The pain of loss is balanced by Christ's love.
Through the tragedy we are brought closer to Christ.
When we are at our weakest,
we are most open to Christ's transforming love.

A Door to the Spiritual World

The tragic on the physical plain opens a door
    to the spiritual world.
It is very painful to walk through that door.
It demands that you purge all illusions and egotistical needs.
But if you have the courage to walk through the door,
transformation and joy begin.

Awe   2/22/07

I have felt God's greatness today,
I am in awe.
I have tasted God's peace today,
I am at rest.
I have sensed God's presence today,
I am in joy!

The Spirit Triumphs Even over Death 2/27/07

We do not understand the essence of the spirit
    until we encounter death.
As all is reduced to nothingness,
a new birth occurs.
Spirit's eternal nature becomes manifest.
We are born again.
Spirit triumphs even over death.
Death leads to new life.
At that moment our faith is tested to the breaking point.
Christ, the Lord of Love, will appear in all His glory.
If we have sought Christ on Earth,
we shall see Him after death.
If we have not sought Him here on Earth,
we will become filled with despair
and have to become determined to seek Him
    in our next earthly life.

Surrounded by Love

How can we fail to notice that we are surrounded by love?
That we are supported in all that we do?
That the very heartbeat that keeps us alive comes
    from an involuntary muscle?
That God's grace is abundant and shines on all of us?

Dream 9: I Read about
Claire's Book Being Published 5/3/07

We were all very happy and joyous and were seated around a table in a room that was filled with luminous midday sunlight. We were in a festive mood. Linda was seated to my left. At the head of the table was Bill. Claire and Ed were opposite Linda and me. Then came Debbie and Bob and John at the other head. Someone else may have been seated next to me, but I could not see that person.

We were all laughing, smiling and engaged in playful teasing. Debbie and I were kidding one another and John kindly asked Debbie to sit next to him. It was very fatherly.

Claire then announced she was going to pour water from this clear pitcher.

I joked, "Don't miss the glass!" Claire laughed and said, "Of course, I have to put it in the glass." Claire smiled and poured the crystalline water from high above her head in a very elegant gesture. The water went down from on high into the glass. Claire smiled and said, "Didn't miss a drop!"

John's elegant, long fingers started leafing through the right side of a stack of letters and counting what he had written. He then put his fingers on the words as if they were braille. On the left side of the letters was a blue book. He was about to read when I woke up.

Part 2: Dream 10: Discernment 5/7/07

I had the following dream last night. I think it is connected with the first one and that they are part of the Whitsun festival we are having in the upper room at The Institute.

I was in a group and the question regarding inner spiritual experiences came up. I stated that I had developed very definite filters that I used to delineate spiritual life and that I had created categories that were boxes. If the experience or person did not fit in the box, I disregarded the experience. I have been trying lately to overcome this bias and let the spirit speak without my filters.

John immediately stood up. John was very calm and deliberate. "I concur with what Neill just stated. It is the nub of the spiritual experience to be open." John held his fingers together to make his point of the nub and then released them to be open. "If we prejudge what the spirit looks like, in whom it will appear, and so on, we are denying the spirit. In fact we are killing the spirit by assuming we know how it should appear." John's gesture was to make an X in the air. "In a certain sense this is an act of spiritual pride. Humility is everything. We don't know how the spirit will appear. We should be open to the spirit. But here is the interesting paradox. We should be open with discernment."

Dream 11: The Cave   7/9/07

I have had a dream for years that I could never remember. I had the dream again and in the dream I realized that something had changed from prior dreams. When I woke up, I recalled the following dream.

I was walking on water, clear green water over a large bay or body of water. I could hear and feel the water splashing when my feet walked on the water. I said to myself, "How can this be that I can walk on water?" I looked down and saw a red brick path a few inches below the water. I then was driving my car over the water as if it were a boat. Again I was amazed that a car could go over water and I assumed there was a brick road underneath, but it did not explain how a car could move through water. I was traveling with Linda, sometimes Nicole, and at one point Debbie.

We arrived at a large cave that was filled with brilliant sunlight as if it did not have a roof and the warm air and sunlight came in unobstructed. The walls were pink with light touches of white. Linda and I walked past the first area and went directly to the second grotto or cave inside the main hall. It was as if these areas were small altars in a grand cathedral. At the second grotto was a golden altar, dazzling to behold. The altar had a vault or safe on the top of the altar in the middle of it. On the vault there was a series of golden knobs and levers that were as beautiful as the altar. If one knew how to work these knobs and levers, the vault would open. I kept starring at the altar and the vault.

There was an angel dressed in a white gown that went to his feet, standing directly in front of the altar. He was masculine in demeanor and was staring at the vault, which he was guarding. I could not resist a joke and said, "I guess there is something pretty important in the vault." All he said was, "Yes." I then asked, " How long have you been here?" "Ages" was his reply.

A small angel then flew past us and then stopped in midair and started flying backward. He seemed like a young boy. I said to Linda, "Look, a flying angel!" Linda said, "You know angels can fly," and nodded to four other angels hovering in midair. They appeared more feminine in nature. They were reprimanding the young angel. "You had better stop flying and learn how to walk. Otherwise your legs will atrophy!" With that, the young angel let down his legs, which he had hidden in his gown. They were undeveloped and he wore black tights over them. He mockingly walked in mid air, taunting the other angels. He laughed at them and said, "Who needs to walk, when you can fly!" And off he flew. The angels then gracefully landed on the ground.

Linda and I then walked back to the first grotto, which was a type of storage area that was half stocked with food and gifts. It was at this point in the dream that I remembered being in this grotto before but it was fully stocked at that point. The difference made me realize I had been here before. I started to pick out some delicious, white peasant bread and dipped it into olive oil and wine. It was fantastic. An angel appeared and I asked, "Are we supposed to pay for this?" The angel replied, "Yes." I asked Linda if she had any money and she looked at me as if I were crazy. "Who would think of bringing money here?" she asked.

We then sheepishly walked away and went into the great hall again. As we walked, I noticed a lion and a lioness on a second floor. The lion started to get on his back legs and was about to roar at us when he stopped. I became concerned but the angels informed us that there was a plastic guard fence separating the lions from us. The animals seemed becalmed. It was as if their natures had become pacified.

We walked past the lions and went to an open area outside the cavern that was like a very large porch. It was ringed with large stones. We beheld a marvelous vista. It was a vast panorama. We could see for miles. The horizon kept growing and it revealed beautiful greens, pinks and other unworldly colors. There were rivers, mountains, and canyons. Each had its own beauty. But it was not the spatial aspect that was most interesting. It was that the view seemed to be of eternity. The view kept expanding.

We then sensed that someone was appearing directly behind us. A person came out of thin air and was born in the spiritual. She was crying and suffering as if she had just died. She was in a fetal position with her hands locked over her eyes. We took a step toward her and four angels surrounded her. They cooed over her as nurses would over a new born babe. Her mood changed with the nursing of the angels. They slowly and gently coaxed her to take her hands off her eyes and then to bring her arms down. They then persuaded and guided her to a standing position. She was like a toddler. They then held her hand and helped her take a step, then two.

Each step they walked with her seemed to be part of a journey in their care of her. She went through different phases from pain to bewilderment to confusion to calmness to acceptance then to joy. Their love for her literally moved her through this process. She was back home.

As we followed the angels of mercy back to the main hall, a jet-black panther with yellow eyes came beside me. Not to fear I said to myself. All I have to do is get past the plastic guard doors and fence. As we approached the door, the panther easily slithered under the door. At this point I decided to pet the panther. I was amazed that its spinal column had ridges. I also realized that the angels had put the plastic there to calm me down about the animals. I prayed that they were right. I then woke up.

This dream had never completely stuck in my memory before this experience of it. I only had small pieces of it in the past. The feeling during and after the dream was mostly of a warm bath of love, calmness, joy, awe and serenity, except of course the parts about the lions and the panther. The dream and reliving it produced a seemingly contradictory soul mood of being awfully humbling. But the two words awfully humbling summarize the experience. Awfully in the sense of full of awe at the depth, breadth and practicality of the love the spiritual worlds have for us, i.e. the angels of mercy nursing us after death. Humbling in that even the smallest experiencing of that love humbles you. We are loved beyond our wildest imaginations and that love is deeply active, personal and practical.

LEARN TO LISTEN   10/25/07

Now you will have to learn how to listen.
You, who love to hear the sound of your own voice.
Be quiet.
Listen.
Do not strain to turn air into words.
Relax into the silence.
Wait and see what happens.
Leave your ego aside.
Listen.

YOU ARE NEVER ALONE   12/19/07

You are never alone.
It may sound impossible,
but it is a spiritual fact.
Just as you were surrounded by amniotic fluid
    in your mother's womb,
you are surrounded by the love of spiritual beings.
You reside in them and they in you.
You are never alone.

Everyone Is Saved

Everyone is saved.
It is only a matter of accepting it.
That acceptance will radiate through you
and change your life.
When each person accepts salvation,
then each person experiences Resurrection.

Prayer Is Incense

Prayer is the incense that rises
   from the inner altar of our souls to God.
It lifts up our hearts to the Lord.
It purifies and opens our spirits.
As it ascends heavenward,
it lifts us out of our sense-bound reality.
It frees our thinking to become meditative and filled with love.
Prayer is the yeast of spiritual life.
With prayer all things rise to the Lord.
It is how our departed loved ones find us.
It provides a channel to us and from us.
It connects the living and the dead.
It is a ray of light that unites Heaven and Earth.
Through a prayerful life, we can turn the Earth into a sun,
shining with the glory of Christ.

PRAYER IS A BALM   4/30/08

Prayer is a balm to the soul.
It calms the raging torments of the heart.
It is the rudder and keel to our small boat.
Prayer is most important in storm-tossed seas.
It brings peace and balance.
Without prayer we are lost at sea,
rudderless and tossed hither and yon
    by the strongest wind or wave.
With prayer we can maintain our course.
With prayer we can find God.

RIVERS OF GRACE   5/14/09, LAS VEGAS

The Earth is bathed in rivers of grace
that flow from the side of the Resurrected Christ.
Each individual can, out of her own free will, enter the river.
This act will begin her transformation into a spiritual
    being of light and love.
The individual will realize that Christ's statements
    are not stern edicts,
but facts of spiritual life that produce joy!
"Love the Lord your God with all your heart
    and with all your soul
and with all your strength and with all your mind." (Mark 12:30)
This is a joyful swimming in the river of grace.
It is not a loss of individuality to do the will of God,
it is joy since His will is to love one another.
Loving God is a release from egotism.
This allows individuals to do what they most earnestly desire,
    "To love your neighbor as your self." (Mark 12:31)
The reborn self loves and by doing so helps transform
    the Earth into a spiritual Sun,
  glowing with love and light.

ȹ

REFLECTIONS ON MORTALITY   6/20/2011

I recently visited my brother Brian who is miraculously still alive, battling stage 4b pancreatic cancer. His victory has a heavy cost: pain, uncertainty, fear, loss of appetite, and an immense dosage of painkillers, which are his daily reality. He sleeps and weeps often. His doctors state that he is a good responder to chemotherapy. The translation from medical speech is that his body can withstand absurd amounts of chemotherapy. The therapy leaves him weak and bed ridden. He has what is called "chemo brain," an inability to concentrate or read.

He has good days and bad days. Concentration is waning and it takes a huge effort of will even to speak haltingly. I phone him often. Conversation is an inherent Reilly characteristic. We live to tell stories. The dialogue is becoming a monologue.

Unfortunately, Elaine, Linda's sister, died recently. Death is ubiquitous. Unlike Brian and Lee, she died suddenly and quickly via a cerebral hemorrhage. Given the charnel activity I have been involved in, my thoughts have turned to mortality.

Excarnation is explicit in incarnation. All that is born, dies. All that dies to the physical is reborn in the spiritual. The spirit that incarnates, takes on flesh, is the same spirit that learns from the flesh. When the spirit has learned all that it can, it leaves the Earth. Why does the spirit of each person take on all the vicissitudes of the flesh? To learn how to love. Why does God create the incredible, symmetrical beauty of the body, the microcosm that reflects the majesty of the macrocosm? To house the spirit, to provide an earthly dwelling, a temple. The body enables us to experience love, freedom and individuality, the trinity of human spirituality.

How can we prove the existence of the spiritual to another individual, especially one on the brink of death? We can't. It would destroy the individual's freedom. Only each person can experience the spirit within the individual soul. The recognition and experience of the spiritual is a gift from the spiritual world. It cannot be won or argued. We can prepare for it, we can seek the spiritual, but the spirit finds us, not the other way around. We have to actively wait.

There are as many paths to the spirit as there are individuals: catharsis, tragedy, reverence, even alcoholism. The key is the seeking and patiently waiting.

Eventually we all return to the spiritual realm. Old age, sickness and death lead us back to our eternal home. Blessed are they who experience the spirit before those three trials. Blessed are they who pray for their loved ones.

TRUST IN YOU, O LORD.

> I put my trust in you, O Lord.
> What other choice do I have?
> I put my faith in you, O Lord.
> What other choice do I have?
> I put my love in you, O Lord.
> What other choice do I have?
> Forgive me, Lord, when I choose to be trustless,
>   faithless and loveless.
> Give me strength, O Lord, to choose You.

℘

Dream 12: A Dream about the Devil Who Looked like George Clooney 9/1/12

I have had many dreams with a theme of encountering the devil. The basic plot is to escape his temptations. They are often extremely realistic and frightening.

This dream entailed a suave, cool, brilliant fellow who looked and had the style of George Clooney in a tuxedo. He was extremely intelligent, way past my intellectual abilities. He oozed confidence. I was outmatched and did not stand a chance against him. He was seductive and you wanted to do his bidding. Resistance was futile.

He looked me straight in the face and at every point in the conversation his charming, smiling face got closer and closer. He used classic sales techniques. Assume the win, close the deal. He asked rhetorical questions that were all aimed at getting me to make a decision and commit to being with him.

He smiled and then acted puzzled. "Neill, I am very busy and I have places to go and people to see. You would not believe how complicated my schedule is. How many times have we met in these encounters?" With that his right hand pushed some etheric keys in a cloud-like computer and up flashed the number 44.

The devil acted shocked. "Forty-four times! We have met forty-four times and you have still not made a decision. That is a waste of time for you and me. We have to come to closure. I would like you to make a decision now." With that closing statement, his face came about a foot away from mine.

I felt undone. I was hollow inside and could offer no resistance. I wanted it over. But a statement came to me in my distress. I did not think it up, it arrived just in the nick of time. I immediately stated it to the devil. "To the best of my knowledge, my father never lied to me." It was as if the words were a fist that smacked him in the face. He jerked backward from the force of the truth. I could sense him cogitating on Tom Reilly and how Tom Reilly was a moral, honest man who never lied to his son, me. The devil seemed dazed and confused. Another line came, which I immediately served to the devil. "And neither has my Heavenly Father!" With that the devil disappeared.

I told this dream experience to a rabbi friend and he stated that Jewish morality is based upon the covenant between Abraham and God and that Jews therefore believe their morality is traced through their fathers back to Abraham and then to God.

EPIPHANIES   1/6/13

We are all in the midst of a mighty battle.
Good and Evil fight for influence over us.
This is an invisible battle, shrouded in mist.
It is not on the physical plane.
It is in the spiritual realm and the heart of each person.
The battle is so loud, so powerful that it silences all else.
Yet this din produces muteness.
The actions are unseen.
The motives are invisible.
Humanity stands in the midst of this battle
and does not comprehend that the battle is for humanity.

Each individual feels the undertow of the struggle.
The battle waxes and wanes.
Whole civilizations are devoured in its maw.
Yet we remain unconscious!
A few brave souls man the walls and hold off total disaster.
Their armor of light shines in the moral decay.
The moral decay is a mighty weapon,
that numbs all spiritual activity.
Doubt, eternal doubt, lames all that it engulfs.
Materialism blinds the spiritual eyes,
intoxicated by the glitter of shiny things.
Our ears are stuffed with meaningless words.
Our ego kneels only to itself.
Darkness rules and makes all distinctions invalid.
Clarity has been seduced by sloth.

But in the midnight of our souls,
we hear the soft sound of the virtues.
Faith, the way we walk with Christ in the darkness.
Hope, the center of our being.
Charity, we forgive and are forgiven for our
    near spiritual death.
Courage, we brave all to find Christ amidst the dross of life.
Truth, we experience the light and love of Christ in our soul.

We realize we are much more than the sum of our fears.
Our mighty foes awaken us to the fact that
    we are essential to God's plan.
The battle is fierce because it is so important.
God has put His faith in us.
We are His best hope.
We must not fail!

"The Kingdom of God Is within You" (Luke 17:21) 4/12/13

"The Kingdom of God is within you."
Everyone who can say "I" has an inner life.
No matter the person's circumstance or position, high or low.
The ability to say "I" delineates the inner world
    from the outer world.
Once the inner world is acknowledged, it grows.
It becomes deeper and wider.
The more you look at it,
the more it grows.
Right before your inner eye,
it expands.
It grows as it expands.
The closer and more detailed your vision,
the more it grows.
It is as if you are looking at the source of growth,
    birth and creativity.

Rejoice! 5/10/13

We rejoice when He calls us by our individual name.
We rejoice when He leads us into His promised land.
We rejoice when He is above us.
We rejoice when He is below us.
We rejoice when He is around us.
We rejoice when He is within us.
Rejoice!

Your First Moral Steps   5/15/13

As a mother hovers over her toddler, watching his first step,
so do I hover over you watching your first moral steps.
The mother is concerned about the inevitable falls,
but rejoices as the child learns to move independently.
Likewise I am deeply concerned
    about your inevitable moral lapses,
but rejoice as you learn to be morally independent.
Both walking and morality demand balance
and have the same goal—freedom.

A Clean Inner Altar   5/30/13

Your inner altar has to be cleansed
    before communion with Me.
For the act of consecration, purity is a critical element.
First the host is transubstantiated.
Then the recipient.
The host is spiritual yeast that transforms the recipient.
But I will always demand a clean, pure inner altar.

A Pure Heart

Purify your heart.
Cleanse your self.
Believe in the Father.
Follow Me.

IN THE MIDST OF ETERNITY 6/1/13

We are walking in the midst of eternity,
yet we know it not.
Our vision is downcast, pedantic.
We await revelation,
yet we seek it not.
Not seeking,
we do not see it.

SEEK ME 6/2/13, Feast of Corpus Christi

I am always awaiting those who seek Me.
Open your eyes.
Call me by My name.
Seek Me.

I HAVE BROUGHT HEAVEN TO EARTH 7/1/13

Now dear children, it is your free task
    to bring Earth to Heaven.

7/10/13

I have a limited understanding of where these songs come from. They are mainly internal, inner experiences. I am suspicious of my own and others undue influence on what I think I am hearing. I try to test them to make sure they are valid. Some times I read or send some to a number of friends to take their read. This has been very helpful.

I do know that I have often been astonished in church. Last Sunday once again we recited Psalm 95:7–8: "If you hear His voice, harden not your heart."

I avoid spiritual activity if I am under the influence of drugs or alcohol. I take pain killers only when necessary and rarely drink. Given that background, it baffles me that after total knee replacement as a pain-ridden, drugged up insomniac I have received an unusual number of songs. They came mostly as I was trying to ambulate, first with a walker, then a cane, and finally walking without any aid. Somehow the effort of trying to walk in spite of the pain opened me up to hear them.

ORIGINAL SIN   7/11/13

"Look at my works, Ye Mighty, and despair."
    (Shelley, *Ozymandias*)
My egotism is the center of my universe.
Please note that I did not state my ego or my "I am."
If I place my egotism at the center of my universe,
it, in essence, becomes my sun.
Or rather my egotism is that around which all else orbits.
I am self-referential, self-defining and self-contained.
This sun-like activity of my egotism blots out everything else.
It is my kingdom, which I populate at my whim.
My egotism determines all: the center of existence, its
    boundaries, the very architecture of the universe.
Thus everything becomes an extension of my egotism.
I, god like, breathe everything into existence.
Or allow it to be.
Control, absolute control, is mine.
I acknowledge no boundaries that I have not created.
I am unfettered.
I am a mirror looking into a sea of mirrors,
enchanted by my own reflections.
Only love, pure non-egotistical love, can cure egotism.

THE DENIAL OF CHRIST'S PRESENCE   7/13/13

My egotism blots out the presence of Christ.
I make Christ occult, hidden.
Christ is manifest.
I undo His manifestation.
If I make Christ hidden,
my egotism is then manifest.
This is the exact opposite of the way of St. John the Evangelist.

John strove to "bear witness" to the eternal,
    loving presence of Christ.
I elect to not "bear witness."
This is my central flaw or sin.
All other sins are bred from this lie,
    the denial of Christ's presence.

THE PATH OF FREEDOM   7/14/13

Who gives us the ability to deny Christ's presence?
Christ.
His love of us is so radical that He gives us
    the capability to deny Him.
This is a non-trivial capability.
Imagine standing outside beneath a resplendent Sun at 12 p.m.
The entire world is enlightened by the Sun.
Imagine the ability to deny the Sun,
to block it from your consciousness.
You would create an eclipse.
This is a glimpse of the power that each individual has.
The ability to deny Christ is a stunning depiction
    of the freedom
that Christ has given to humanity.
This freedom is the essence of Christ's loving relationship
    with us.
Imagine if that capability were used to affirm
    the presence of Christ.
An individual's relationship with Christ is a direct
    proof of her freedom.
If she affirms Christ,
she is on the path of freedom.
If she denies Christ,
she is on the path of slavery.

CHRIST AS THE LOGOS   7/15/13

Let us assume that Christ is the Logos, the Alpha
    and the Omega.
If such, he is the Creator and Redeemer of reality.
He is Lord of All.
If so He will be the most realistic of all beings,
since He has created reality.
As The Creator, His words and deeds would be
    the most important events
in the history of the world and humanity.
Christ would be the most practical of all beings.
He would know precisely the ramifications of all thoughts,
    words and deeds.
If He is The Redeemer and Creator,
it would serve us well to listen and follow Him.

CONSUMED BY PAIN   7/27/13

I am consumed by my pain.
Pain is ubiquitous and dominates my consciousness more than
    my own thoughts.
New pain, old pains, slight variations on intensity.
Pain most of the time, days and nights.
Drugs reduce the pain, but lead to other problems.
Night pain reigns supreme,
No position in bed works.
Sleeplessness robs the healing power of sleep.
Day seems better,
but does not conquer pain, only mitigates it.
My ego is swamped by the pain.
I am tasting mortality and it is bitter.
Mother Therese stated, "Be humble or be prepared
    to being humbled."
I am being humbled.

THE ENDLESS LOVE OF CHRIST

There is only one ever-loving, ever-truthful, ever-beautiful,
    ever-good reality: Christ.
As the Sun emanates all light,
its rays penetrate the deepest darkness.
So does Christ's love penetrate the coldest heart,
inflaming it with love.
Nothing can withstand the endless love of Christ.
Eventually, even if it is at the far edge of eternity,
Christ's love will transform all.
Of this we can be sure and rejoice, "Come, sweet Redeemer."

IMAGINE!

Imagine that God loved you so much that He gave you
    a personal invitation to Genesis!
That He not only wanted you present at Creation,
    but wanted you to participate in Creation!

1   In the beginning was the Word, and the Word was with
    God, and the Word was God.
2   The same was in the beginning with God.
3   All things were made by Him; and without Him was not
    any thing made that was made.
4   In Him was Life; and the Life was the Light of men.
5   And the Light shineth in darkness; and the darkness
    comprehended it not. (John 1:1–5)

Imagine that Christ loved you so much that He would Incarnate, live through His Passion and Crucifixion and then Resurrect. That He would do all this so that you could freely unite with Him.

14 And the Word was made flesh, and dwelt among us, (and
we beheld his glory, the glory as of the only begotten of the
Father,) full of grace and truth. (John 1:14)

Imagine that Christ loved you so much that no matter how
often you abandoned Him, He would never abandon you.

20 I am with you always, even unto the end of the world.
(Matt. 28:20)

CREATION IS NOT FINISHED   8/3/13

How sad, truly tragic, if we believe creation is finished!
Then everything is done, fixed, finished and final.
The wheels of entropy will grind everything into the dust.
The logic of defeatism and negativity will rule.
There will be no hope.
Christ, The Lord of Creation, makes all things new.

THOMAS AND PAUL

We are all modern, materialistic thinkers.
That is how it is meant to be until we experience Christ.
We all have Occam's razor between our left and right ears.
"The simplest solution is often the best."
Our materialistic thinking tends toward simplicity
and, more exactly, superficiality.
It is so much easier to think simple, superficial thoughts.
Or better yet, to not even think at all.
When we approach life, our implicit assumptions
        about the nature of reality
become the glasses through which we look.
We perceive only that which is within the realm
        of our consciousness.

Our first step as modern, empirical materialists is
    to have unbiased observations.
This is actually very hard to do.
We all approach phenomena with prejudgment.
We assume we know.
Better to assume we do not know and just observe.
Let the phenomena speak.
Let the concept emerge from the percept.
They are one.
We have split them.
We need to re-member them.
Inner silence is critical.
This silence builds the altar upon which mysteries can unfold.
No silence, no altar, no mysteries.
That is why modern life is so noisy.
The physical clatter blots out the silence
    and hence the spiritual.
Since we are spiritual beings in a spiritual world,
we are granted spiritual percepts all the time.
We often lack the concepts to unite with the percepts.
Therefore, the spiritual percept passes us by.
Just as the apostles slept through Christ's agony in the garden,

Think of Thomas and Paul.
They were exactly like us.
They believed as they were taught to believe.
They thought as they were taught to think.
When Thomas was not physically present for the resurrected,
    spiritual body of Christ,
Thomas gave the most honest, human answer.
He was an empirical, scientific materialist.
"Except I shall see in his hands the print of the nails,
    and put my finger into the print of the nails, and thrust
    my hand into his side, I will not believe. " (John 20:25)

We are all Thomas.
Christ then manifested Himself to Thomas and Thomas was
    made new.
Thomas did not put his hand into Christ's side.
Thomas apprehended the Risen Christ and gave the ultimate
    recognition,
"My Lord and My God!"

Paul was even more severe in his denial of Christ.
Paul was a scourge of the early Christians.
The risen Christ then manifested Himself to Paul.
Paul had an intimate and complete conversion.
So radical was Paul's conversion that he became the most
    dynamic of all missionaries.
Paul never stopped introducing others to Christ.

We are all modern Thomases and Pauls.

SPIRITUAL AVOIDANCE   8/13/13

Why do I avoid You?
Seek darkness and shadows over Your Light?
Why do I twist and turn the truth to fit my desires?
Why do I resist You?
What would be easier or more beneficial than
    to acknowledge You
and bring You into my heart of hearts?
How can I be so weak and foolish?

YOUR SOFT, SOFT VOICE   8/16/13

If I sometimes quiet my self
I may hear your soft, soft voice.
Soft, yet it fills all of me.

I listen to its sweet cadence.
Like a loved one's voice,
it has depth and resonance.
Our very selves are carried in the tone of our voices.
My interior feels your warmth and love.
How does such a soft voice
have such a powerful impact?

ARMOR OF LIGHT   9/4/13

I have a recurring image that we are all in the midst of a
    karmic vortex.
We have sworn allegiance to the Light,
but matters seem to be spinning out of control.
There is a palpable sense of guilt that we have failed to meet
    the challenge.
We have forgotten or forsaken our sacred vows to be bearers of
    the Light.
The darkness seems to swirl around us and mock us.
Individuals we know seem lost and transfixed, blinded by
    materialism.
Ourselves included!
We fear to speak of what we know.
We cower.
We are craven about the spirit when we need to be brave and
    courageous.
The world seems mad and incoherent.
Syria looms as a harbinger.
It is abundantly clear that we need communion with Christ.
"The night is far spent, the day is at hand: let us therefore
    cast off the works of darkness and let us put on the
    armor of light." (Rom. 13:12)

THE SEED AND THE PLANT   10/6/13

Is the seed the apotheosis of the plant?
Or is the plant the apotheosis of the seed?
Our cause and effect cognition wants a sequential answer.
But what if the seed and the plant are one?
And we are missing the whole by slicing it into cause and effect.
What if by demanding sequential logic,
     we are obfuscating eternity?
What if the seed is more important than cause and effect?
What if the seed contains all that is plant
and the plant contains all that is seed?
What if seed and plant abide within one another?
Could the seed free us from mere cause and effect linear logic?

LOVE MAKES ALL THINGS ANEW   10/14/13

The dogma of faith has been replaced by
     the ideology of materialism.
Both dogma and ideology deny freedom of thinking.
While dogma and ideology are necessary for group thinking,
they tend toward calcification and rigidity.
They provide a logical paradigm for defining reality.
Yet the strength of dogma and ideology is also their weakness.
In creating a strong architectural foundation,
     they lose the flow of the spirit.
The spiritual realm is constantly evolving,
     moving from seed to plant to flower to seed.
Spirit is the flower that grows in the crack in concrete.
Spirit is evolution in movement. It is dance and song.
Spirit is love.
And love is never stagnant and formulaic.
     It is dynamic and creative.
Love makes all things anew including dogma and ideology.

FAITH, HOPE AND CHARITY   1/6/14

Each day we can choose denial or Faith.
Choose Faith!
Each day we can choose despair or Hope.
Choose Hope!
Each day we can choose hate or Charity.
Choose Charity!
We must not yield to denial.
We must not descend to despair.
We must not succumb to hate.
May we abide in Faith, Hope and Charity.

THE LIGHT OF CHRIST   3/2/14

God has given each of us a task,
a mission to bring His Light to darkness.
Spiritual Light to our darkness and the darkness of the world.
Physical light brings material objects into view.
We do not see light,
we see through or because of light.
When the Sun sets, darkness ensues.
We lose our physical sight.
Spiritual Light brings spiritual being into view.
We do not see spiritual light,
we see spiritual reality because of His Light.
When the Light of Christ arises, darkness retreats.
We gain our spiritual sight.

ASH WEDNESDAY 3/5/14

We are all going to die.
We do not know when and how.
This thought can be depressing or enlightening.
Before we face death,
acceptance of mortality is critical.
To be mortal is humbling.
We are not demigods,
yet we act as if we are.
Hubris.
It is very hard to imagine a world before
or after our own existence.
Therein lies the rub.
Clearly the world existed before us
and will exist after our demise.
How humbling!
Or how truthful.
The journey in Lent is through the Passion and Death
    to Resurrection.
The internal image is resplendent.
We shed the physical and return to the spiritual.
Life, spiritual life, survives physical death.
We die to become.

THE SHELL OF EGOTISM 4/15/14

We carry our egotism,
    as a tortoise carries his shell.
Egotism serves us in certain situations,
    just as the hard shell protects the tortoise.
If we retreat into the darkness of our egotism too often,
    we cut ourselves off from life.
Yes, we are secure in our egotism.

Egotism is as familiar as an old shoe.
It is comfortable and sure fitting.
Egotism forms a cave around us,
insulating us from all others.
We do not need to completely lose our egotism.
But like a lobster, we could molt into a softer shell.
Maybe, just maybe, we can try to put others before ourselves.
Worth a try.

The Balm to Egotism   8/2/14

Our egotism is like a net.
It captures us, ensnares us in our own devices.
We are bound, hand and foot.
The more we struggle,
the tighter the net becomes.
We are entombed within our own egotistical universe,
like a nut in a shell.
We are isolated and removed from all others.
We live in a solipsistic daze.
Who can free us from ourselves?
Who can free our egos from our egotism?
Christ freely offers us the balm to egotism.
"Love the Lord your God with all your heart
    and with all your soul
and with all your strength and with all your mind.
Love your neighbor as yourself." (Mark 12:30–31)

OUR FATHER   6/5/94, 8/21/14

Our Father, Everyone's Father, not My Father.
More Dad or Daddy. Think of a Jewish child saying Abba,
who art in Heaven.
Dad's home is in Heaven.
We, his sons and daughters, are away from home.
We are the prodigal sons and daughters.
Hallowed be Thy name.
God's name is holy. Even speaking His name is special,
    a spiritual experience.
Like Moses, we need to take our sandals off.
Thy kingdom come.
The purpose of earthly existence is to bring
    our Father's kingdom or presence into being on this Earth.
This is the second coming.
Thy will be done.
His will is Love.
The way to do it is by opening ourselves to His will, His Love.
Think of Mary opening her self to God's will,
    "I am the handmaiden of the Lord." (Luke 1:38)
Think of Christ, "Not as I will, but as Thou will." (Matt. 26:39)
On Earth as it is in Heaven.
The two will be reunited by doing His will.
Give us this day our daily bread.
We need to be sustained physically and spiritually.
We need manna, we need communion.
"I am the bread of life." (John 6:35)
And forgive us our trespasses.
Everyone wants and needs forgiveness.
As we forgive those who trespass against us.
Here is the hard part. If we ask for mercy,
    how can we deny others mercy?
To be forgiven, we must forgive.

"Father, forgive them, for they know not what they do."
    (Luke 23:34)
And lead us not into temptation.
Do not give us a cross beyond our strength.
But deliver us from evil.
We are weak and likely to fail.
If we do fail, help us recover.
For thine is the kingdom and the power and the glory forever.
Your kingdom, (presence), power and glory shall last forever.
Guide us into your eternal love
    that we may forever share in your grace.

Amen.

CATHARSIS AIN'T FUN   9/9/14

Our ego has 2 polar opposite tendencies.
The first is egotistical.
The second is communal.
They constantly conflict with one another.
Should I be an individual who caters only to my self?
Or should I dedicate my self to God and others?
This internal civil war divides our ego
    into the egotistical and the I am.
Egotism is of the moment.
The I Am is eternal.

THE DIVINE SONG   10/5/14

God loved the world so much,
He had to sing the world into existence.
His love was so great,
He had to create.
His divine love and divine will are one.
His song of creation is one of love and harmony.
When we are in accord with His love and will,
we become co-creators with Him.
We join His song of creation.
And sing His praises.

STEP OUT OF THE DARKNESS   10/22/14

Step out of the darkness of our own egotism.
Step into the abundant sunshine of Christ's love and light.
We often prefer the darkness to sunshine.
We feel safe and comfortable in our darkness.
Light, the transparent light of Christ's love,
      reveals all and transforms all.
Our darkest deeds, thoughts and feelings become apparent.
We shudder in shame
and shutter our hearts and souls.
Just as we cannot forever hide from the rays of the Sun,
we cannot forever hide from the light of Christ's love.
His love seeks out the darkest places,
even the darkness of the human heart.
And just as all plants grow toward the Sun,
all humans grow toward the Son.

DREAM 13: STANDING ON A LEDGE   11/1/14

I dreamt that I was standing on a ledge. The ledge was on a sheer cliff that arose into the clouds. The cliff was steeper than the Grand Canyon, overlooking a vast vista. Down below was the Earth. It was majestic in its green blue beauty. I loved the Earth and all that inhabited it. I wanted to be there, but not yet.

Above and behind the ledge were angelic beings. I could not see them. I could only sense them. I had the feeling that they were watching me. I was being observed just as I was observing the Earth. It was more of being beheld than being watched. The angels behold humanity. Their angelic beholding affirms our spiritual existence. This is in direct contrast to Descartes' famous intellectual statement, "Cogito ergo sum," "I think therefore I am." Their beholding of humans affirms the spiritual reality of each individual human. We are beheld, therefore we exist as distinct spiritual beings.

There was a conversation that I was overhearing. My self-appointed tasks were to listen to the conversation, to sense that we are indebted to their watching us and to look at and love the Earth. Since the conversation was above and behind, it was very difficult to hear. We have to strain to hear it.

We out of freedom allow their grace to flow through us to the Earth. They cannot command us to do this free act. In fact, it would pervert their love. The angelic beings cannot reach across the void and connect with the Earth. They need us to transform the Earth.

Saint Theresa of Avila stated "Christ has no body now but yours. No hands, no feet on Earth but yours. Yours are the eyes through which he looks with compassion on this world. Yours are the feet with which he walks to do good. Yours are the hands through which he blesses the entire world. Yours are the hands, yours are the feet, yours are the eyes, you are his body. Christ has no body now on Earth but yours."

We are destined to become co-creators of a new Earth with them. Ironically, the microcosm has to save the macrocosm.

℘

"SEEK AND YE SHALL FIND" (LUKE 11:9)   5/2/2015

We are all drunk on egotism.
We have taken mighty draughts of self-interest.
We blind ourselves to anything beyond our own
    egotistical desires.
Like a King or an Emperor, we serve only ourselves.
We look to expand our kingdom's borders.
We are asleep to anything beyond our own interests.
Our blindness is so total, we stumble through life.
Fortunately, we fall.
Our own blindness leads to a shameful realization.
We are sleep-walking.
We perceive our errors as extensions of our selves.
We are humbled by the children of our actions.
We are aware that we are unconscious.
How do we steer our ship without a rudder?
How do we pick a course without a compass?
What can we do?
We start to seek.
Newton's apple falling to the ground is
    a repeatable experiment.
Each person can perform the act and get the same result.
Likewise we can apply Christ's statement in
    "the smithy of our souls."

It can be tried and verified by each individual.

It is not subjective: it is objective.

There is no bias, unprejudiced observation will test its reality.

Once proven, it becomes a spiritual theory of identity, A=A.

The above quotation by Christ is declarative and axiomatic.

There is nothing conditional about it.

It is a spiritual fact.

It is the fulcrum to move the universe.

But what or whom do we seek and what or whom do we find?

Could it be understood that we seek Him and that allows us
to find Him?

Is it that simple?

Could it possibly be true?

If your daughter sought your help,

wouldn't you do everything in your power to help her find you?

"For My Yoke Is Easy
and My Burden Is Light" (Matt. 11:30)   11/6/15

You have made life too complicated.

Yes, life can be dense and confusing, almost kaleidoscopic.

Some use this chaos as an excuse for irresponsibility.

"I don't understand" is not an acceptable way to navigate life.

Each of you has an inner life.

It is far richer than you imagine.

Each of you can reach Me through your inner life.

You can gain understanding, if you but try.

Do you have a better answer?

"Abide in Me as I Abide in You" (John 15:4)   11/7/15

I will never abandon you.
I am always with you.
Your freedom and love connect us.
If you act in freedom and love,
you will find me.
I joyfully await you.

Inner experiences

How should we consider inner experiences?
Are dreams, imaginations and intuitions real?
How can we put them to the test?
Are they will-o'-the-wisps that evaporate
    like the morning mist?
Or do they persist?
Do they lead to awe, reverence and gratitude?
Where do they come from?
How do they manifest themselves?
Do we create them or are they guests that visit us?

Every child

Every child who moves from "Mary wants ice cream"
to "I want ice cream" has experienced
    the beginning of the incarnation of the "I Am."
This is a precious and often unseen moment
    of the greatest import.
The inner life has manifested itself to itself.

IMPORTANT ACTIVITY

One of the most important activities
    you are going to do today is praying.
Prayer will center your day
and the way you meet the world.
All of life is a prayer.

HEAVEN

Acceptance of My presence is Heaven.
Heaven is not a place, a state or a time.
Heaven is Now.
Denial of My presence is hell.
Your choice.

A MIRROR

Think of a person you dislike.
Hold her in your imagination.
Work on it.
Does she share some of your faults?
Is she really that disagreeable?
Can you learn from her to smooth your own edges?

REMEMBER ME

Remember Me,
as I remember you.
I never forget you,
even for an instant.
As a mother gazes lovingly on her sleeping babe,
so do I behold you.

"WITH GOD ALL THINGS ARE POSSIBLE" (MATT. 19:26)   1/15/16

This statement could appear to be absurd, unrealistic.

Who would make such a declaration?

The Logos who is in the presence of God's creativity.

Who vanquished death and demonstrated the eternity of the
spirit via the Resurrection.

Let us assume we are made in the image and likeness of God.

What an assumption!

What if we had the god-like ability to predict the future?

Better yet, what if we had the ability to directly influence
events in the future?

We do.

Terms like karma and fate are so misunderstood.

Life is not deterministic.

Life only appears fixed.

All future possibilities have the potential to become realized.

God is free to make all things possible.

Time and space are materialistic subsets of His creation.

It is His precious freedom that He gives to us.

We, consciously or unconsciously, make our own fate, our own
karma.

Once we begin to understand the mighty, awesome, humbling
responsibility of freedom, we can try to act more
consciously like Christ, the knowing doer,

who loves all existence, physical and spiritual, into being.

SPIRITUAL ACTIVITY IS INCENSE   2/15/16

Spiritual activity is incense,
rising to the heavens.
Spiritual activity declares our existence
    and location to spiritual beings,
including the so-called dead.
Spiritual activity is a buoy.
It creates a marker for where we are.
Once the spiritual world knows we exist and where we are,
it can shower grace upon grace upon us.
Spiritual activity is the free act that connects us
    to the spiritual world.
We are open and the spiritual world fills us up.
By seeking, we are found.

SEEK   2/19/16

Seek the Good.
Seek the Truth.
Seek the Beautiful.
Seek, seek, seek.

Prayer Connects Us

Through prayer we can become connected with Our Father.
In fact we are already connected with Our Father.
It is just that we are asleep.
There is a spiritual umbilical cord between us and Our Father.
It is a clear, translucent light.
It surrounds us and connects us all together.
Spirit connects to spirit, flesh to flesh.
We can open this connection and receive even more love.
Just as the Word became flesh,
our task is make the flesh become the Word.
The Incarnation allowed us to know
we are spiritual children of God.
Now we can use the umbilical cord of love and light
and be born again.

Spark of Divinity

We all have a spark of divinity within us.
If used improperly, this spark can inflame egotism,
pride and arrogance.
If guarded properly, it can grow into spirit self.
Is the spirit self the same as the ego?
Or does the ego serve the spirit self?

The Next Thing   4/23/16

Do not look to jump from one thing to the next.
Stay with what is in front of you.
You are not meant to be endlessly distracted,
floating hither and yon.
Rather, you are most yourself
when you are at one with your spirit self.
You will be amazed.

LISTEN   4/30/16

Listen,
in the core of your being.
Listen,
in your heart of hearts.
Listen,
for the guest at the door.
Listen.

THE SPIRITUAL WORLD IS TRANSPARENT   5/1/16

The spiritual world is transparent.
It is invisible to the physical eye.
Just as we don't see air,
we don't see the spirit.
Like air, it is everywhere there is life.
Without air, we die.
Likewise without the spirit, we die.
We don't see light.
We see because of light.
We see through the light.
We see and breathe through the gift of the spirit.
We live and breathe in the spirit.
The spirit is transparent to us.
Yet it is the source of all being.

THE MOST IMPORTANT ACTIVITY   7/3/16

What is the most important activity you will do today?
Could it be your morning prayer?
Your prayer aligns your will with My will.
Your prayer opens the door between Heaven and Earth.
Your prayer reunites us.
Your prayer balances you for all you will encounter today.

Why Do We Reincarnate? 8/8/16

It is easy to become world-weary.
Wars, sickness, old age and poverty can almost
    extinguish our individual souls.
Yet time and again, we reincarnate.
Why?
Why do we bother?
Wouldn't it be easier to stay in the spiritual realm,
our home, and not have to deal with all this suffering?
The reasons we incarnate are manifold and individualistic.
Mainly it comes down to loving our family,
    friends and the Earth itself.
We want to remain connected with loved ones and the Earth.
But above all that love,
we return to the Earth to connect with Christ,
the source of all love and being.

Incarnation 10/6/16

We do not remember creating our bodies.
If we did create them,
we are unconscious of the act.
We also do not remember asking our hearts to beat.
Or asking our lungs to supply air to our bodies.
The term involuntary muscle should apply to most of our body.
Our bodies have a wisdom beyond our ken.
Our bodies have an inherent rhythm, symmetry and beauty
that makes them the masterpieces of creation.
All that creation to house each individual spirit.

SPIRITUAL AMNESIA
10/23/16

We have forgotten everything
we ever knew of the spiritual.
We are adrift, rudderless,
without any sense of direction.
From this chaos,
we resolve to seek.
From this meaninglessness,
we affirm meaning.
We are seekers, freedom fighters,
fools who believe in meaning.
We will to feel the presence of Christ.

THE LOGOS AND GENESIS
11/9/16

The Logos creates creativity.
The Logos comes before creativity.
The Logos pours itself out into Genesis.
Genesis comes before space and time.
The Creator comes before creation.
Creation comes before the created.
"I am the Alpha and the Omega,
the first and the last, the beginning and the end." (Rev. 22:13)

GENESIS

What tense should we use for Genesis?
Is it the past?
Or perhaps, it is the eternal present, Now.
Does Genesis have an end?
Or is it constantly evolving and creating?
Genesis is the never-ending song.

SPIRITUAL ELITISM   11/25/16

Spiritual elitism is a sin.
We convince ourselves that we are the elect.
We proceed with the perspective that we are God's chosen.
This can justify any absurd rationalization
from slavery to war.
In fact we are all sinners and saints.
We are all part of the mystical body of Christ.
Every single individual is precious to the Lord.
We somehow forget this in our egotism.
In our egotism we deny that the best translation
of Christ's use of *Abba* is the plural possessive pronoun,
   "Our Father."
These two words immediately state the spiritual fact.
We are all children of God.

THE ETERNAL NOW, THE ETERNAL PRESENT   12/4/16

If Christ is the Logos, he exists before space and time.
Eternity exists before, during and after time.
Temporal time only exists after the Sun is created.
Time is a subset of eternity.
Perhaps it is more fitting to consider using
   the Eternal Present with Christ.

1   In the beginning is the Word, and the Word is with God,
    and the Word is God.
2   The same is in the beginning with God.
3   All things are made by him; and without him is not any
    thing made that is made.
4   In him is life; and the life is the light of men.
5   And the light shines in darkness; and the darkness
    comprehends it not.

6 There was a man sent from God, whose name was John.

7 The same came for a witness, to bear witness of the Light, that all men through him might believe.

8 He was not that Light, but was sent to bear witness of that Light.

9 That is the true Light, which lighteth every man that cometh into the world.

10 He is in the world, and the world is made by him, and the world knows him not.

11 He comes unto his own, and his own receives him not.

12 But as many as receive him, to them gives he power to become the sons of God, even to them that believe on his name:

13 Which are born, not of blood, nor of the will of the flesh, nor of the will of man, but of God.

14 And the Word is made flesh, and dwells among us (and we behold His glory, the glory as of the only begotten of the Father) full of grace and truth.

15 John bore witness of Him, and cried, saying, "This was He of whom I spake, He that cometh after me is preferred before me: for He was before me."

16 And of His fullness do all we receive, and grace for grace.

17 For the law was given by Moses, but grace and truth come by Jesus Christ.

18 No man hath seen God at any time, the only begotten Son, which is in the bosom of the Father, He declares Him.

(John 1:1–18)

How Many Times? 12/8/16

How many times a day do we forget Thee, O Lord?
We get enmeshed in the flotsam and jetsam of daily life.
We forget grace before meals, thanksgiving after meals
and praise of your creation.
How is it that we so easily forget Thee?
Why is it such an effort to stay awake
and to remember You?

Encountering Death 12/12/16

Encountering death is a sobering experience.
We meet our future and are repelled by its finality.
We lose a loved one and are properly bereft.
The conversation has ended.
An ineluctable silence ensues.
All seems finished.
But, if we persevere, we may find it is not a total silence.
This stillness fosters a receptivity in our grief.
It is a quickening of the essential.

Without Christ 12/29/16

Without Christ we are stuck in the finite.
There is no star to guide our boat.
There is no eternal Truth or Beauty or Goodness.
They become mere words, concepts without any reality.
Empty ideas to be argued over.
The concept of relativity has moved from physics to morality.
Everything is just a perception, an opinion.
Life begins at birth and ends at death.
Period.

With Christ we are part of the infinite.
We are connected with every person, action,
    idea and feeling we encounter.
We behold eternal Truth, Beauty and Goodness.
They are not mere words.
They are realities we can dwell in.
By dwelling in them, we evolve.
We become more Christlike.
By His incarnation, Christ has demonstrated that
    life has intrinsic meaning.
Even an inglorious crucifixion leads to a glorious Resurrection.

FREEDOM AND RESPONSIBILITY   12/31/16

Do we know that the spiritual world exists?
Better yet, does the spiritual world know that we exist?
How can the spiritual world know or acknowledge
    our presence,
if we do not know or acknowledge its presence?
Imagine going to a party and not knowing anyone's name,
walking through a group of people and not even looking
    in their eyes.
If we do not encounter the spiritual world,
it cannot encounter us.
If we avoid the spiritual encounter,
our denial will lead to tragic, karmic consequences.
We own our own spiritual path.
Our spiritual responsibility determines our fate.
This is the hallmark of freedom:
Individual responsibility for our own karma.

DENIAL OF THE SPIRIT   1/9/17

You just don't get it.
You foolishly waste time and energy.
You have this immense spiritual potential inside you.
You ignore it at your own risk.
Recall World War I.
It could have been stopped by a few, awakened individuals.
The tragic is not fate.
The denial of the spirit produces the tragic.
Your choice is self-imposed catharsis or outer imposed tragedy.
Make your choice.

DOUBT AND FAITH   1/3/17

Doubt is the cornerstone of faith.
What?
Humans are plagued by doubt.
Doubting is an inherent part of human nature.
Beyond mathematics, there are very few certainties.
We have to traverse doubts,
meeting them again and again and again.
To be human is to doubt ourselves, God and reality.
We doubt our own experiences.
We wonder, "Is this real? Am I imagining this?
    Am I deluding myself?"
If we do not exert our wills,
doubts can cripple us.
If we face our doubts,
they can shrink and we can grow.
Doubts are the fire that temper the steel of our faith.

In My Darkness   1/17/17

In the darkness of my soul,
I can pray.
In the darkness of my thoughts,
I can pray.
In the darkness of my outer life,
I can pray.
Darkness and prayers are cause and effect
    in the spiritual world.

Only with Christ   1/24/17

If I destroy everything,
I will rule the world.
There is a tendency in each individual to rule.
Not only to rule, but to rule supreme.
Even if by ruling, all else is destroyed,
creating a wasteland of nothing over which I rule.
This destructive tendency is real and powerful.
It is very dangerous.
It cannot be countered with logic or will.
Only with love.
Only with Christ.

A Subtle Song   1/27/17

How can we accept that loved ones die and leave us?
Or that we will die and leave loved ones?
If we are strictly materialistic,
there is no definitive proof of an afterlife.
Sense-bound thinking cannot penetrate to the spiritual realms.
But this darkness impels us to search for the light.
Are we children of a harsh God?
Are we a random fluke of everlasting chaos?
Is there a subtle song weaving throughout creation?
A song that demands our stillness and quietude.
From our inner darkness, a song can arise
    that brings forth light.

Praying when Sick

I do not like to pray or meditate when I am sick.
I lack concentration, the ability to stay with a thought
    or an image.
All seems chaotic, diffuse, almost kaleidoscopic.
Any small diversion can take me off my course.
All the more important to persevere.

Daily Spiritual Activity   2/11/17

Are we too busy for daily spiritual activity?
Are praying, meditating and reading so onerous?
Are we so busy with our daily responsibilities,
our getting and spending?
Are we captains of our own boats,
or are we buffeted by each and every wind, hither and yon?
Steiner states that each individual is responsible
    for her own spiritual evolution.
Our karma is self determined.

Imagine you had a friend you never visited,
    never spoke with, never thought of.
The relationship would die.
Likewise if we never connect with spiritual beings in this life,
they cannot connect with us.
There is no relationship.
When we go to the spiritual realm,
they don't know us.
Steiner states, even two minutes of spiritual activity a day
    is helpful.
Two minutes!

"SEEK AND YE SHALL FIND" (LUKE 11:9)   2/11/17

Christ's statement is declarative and filled with love and
    spiritual reality.
We can often moan.
"Why is this happening to me?
Why doesn't Christ release me from this situation?"
The answer is difficult to accept.
We created this problem.
We arranged our karma to experience it.
But more importantly is that Christ loves our freedom so much.
Freedom is the essence of an individual.
Christ died to initiate us into spiritual freedom.
If He manifested Himself or came into our lives
    without our invitation,
He would obliterate our freedom.
He would nullify His own Resurrection.
We would be unfree.
He loves us so much that He awaits our loving Him
    in freedom.
We have to actively seek Him to find Him.

"Abide in me as I abide in you."

(John 15:4)

Bibliography

Bamford, Christopher. *The Voice of the Eagle: The Heart of Celtic Christianity.* Great Barrington, MA: Lindisfarne Books, 2001.

Hadfield, Chris. *An Astronaut's Guide to Life on Earth: What Going to Space Taught Me about Ingenuity, Determination, and Being Prepared for Anything.* New York: Little, Brown, 2013.

Steiner, Rudolf. *Becoming the Archangel Michael's Companions: Rudolf Steiner's Challenge to the Younger Generation.* Great Barrington, MA: SteinerBooks, 2006.

———. *From Jesus to Christ.* London: Rudolf Steiner Press, 1991.

———. *Intuitive Thinking as a Spiritual Path: A Philosophy of Freedom.* Hudson, NY: Anthroposophic Press, 1995.

———. *Karmic Relationships: Esoteric Studies,* vol. 3. London: Rudolf Steiner Press, 1977.